Good Housekeeping
Consumer Guide

Buying &
Selling
Your Home

Good Housekeeping
Consumer Guide

Buying &
Selling
Your Home

Jane Brazier

EBURY PRESS · LONDON

First published in 1995

1 3 5 7 9 10 8 6 4 2

First published in the United Kingdom in 1995 by
Ebury Press · Random House · 20 Vauxhall Bridge Road · London SW1V 2SA

Random House Australia (Pty) Limited
20 Alfred Street · Milsons Point · Sydney · New South Wales 2061 · Australia

Random House New Zealand Limited
18 Poland Road · Glenfield
Auckland 10 · New Zealand

Random House South Africa (Pty) Limited
PO Box 337 · Bergvlei · South Africa

Random House UK Limited Reg. No. 954009

A CIP catalogue record for this book is available from the British Library.

Editor: Alison Wormleighton
Design: Martin Lovelock

ISBN: 0 09 180698 4

Printed and bound in Great Britain by Clays Limited, St Ives, plc.

Contents

Introduction

Most people approach buying and selling a home with a mixture of excitement and confusion. It has been said that it is the third most stressful experience, preceded only by a family bereavement and divorce. This guide aims to take the stress out of the process, providing you with a clear vision of the stages of buying and selling a home.

A house purchase is probably the single greatest investment you will make, with a financial commitment for anything up to 25 years, but unlike many other purchases you do not have the same comeback if anything goes wrong. The guide explains all the costs you can expect to encounter and steps to take to ensure you are making the right choice with your money.

If you can't seem to track down your 'dream home', the chapter on self-build gives you an introduction into having your own individual home built.

The guide covers all aspects of the property market including a chapter explaining the legal system for buying and selling in Scotland, which differs from that in England, Wales and Northern Ireland.

At the back the guide includes a comprehensive list of contacts and organisations willing to help you.

The all-important point for a stress-free move is to keep yourself organised. General tips include filing all documents and keeping copies of all correspondence.

With the help of this guide you will be able to consider all possibilities whether it be contracting a professional or simply finding someone to disconnect the washing machine. With the help provided, the buying and selling of your home will run smoothly as a result of good judgement rather than just good luck.

CHAPTER 1

Buying a House or Flat

COSTS OF MOVING

People move for a variety of reasons, particularly employment relocation or the size of the present house. Maybe there isn't enough space for a growing family, or perhaps retirement only demands a small house.

Whatever the reason, there are certain factors you need to consider once you've decided to move house.

Budgeting for the move

Before embarking on house-hunting you need to get the overall costs of moving into perspective and consider the budget you can allow for the new house.

After careful consideration you may feel it would be more worthwhile to improve the house you're in, if possible, to give you more space and facilities. But bear in mind that the costs of extensions or alterations are not likely to be recouped by an increase in value when you eventually come to sell.

Unless you are a first-time buyer, the normal procedure these days, with a slow housing market, is to put off looking for your new house until you are fairly sure of a buyer for the existing home. There is no point in setting your heart on a dream house if you can't sell your old one. Most people need to sell first to release the money from one house to finance the move.

How much can you afford?

Once you've decided to move, approach an estate agent, who will give you an idea of the value of your house.

The Cost of Moving House

What expenses are there when moving house? As well as paying the face value of a house, other transactions need to be budgeted for:

- Deposit
- Stamp Duty
- Mortgage fees
- House-hunting
- Legal costs - plus searches and surveys
- Removals

Negative equity – your options

When the value of your house is now less than the mortgage you are paying on it, as a result of falling house prices, you are in a negative equity position. If you try to sell your house it will not generate enough to pay off the mortgage you have.

There are two main options open to you:

- You can wait until there is an upturn in the market, when house prices will rise and you will be able sell at a reasonable price to fund purchasing a new house.
- You can sell your house and take the value of the negative equity with you.

Many lenders have negative equity schemes available to their customers. The most common one adds the negative equity on to the new mortgage. You take a loan at 125 per cent instead of the usual 95 per cent maximum. This type of negative equity mortgage consists of a 95 per cent loan on the new property and another loan to cover the negative equity on the old property.

The additional loan is unsecured or alternatively the lender may take the equity of your parents' home into account as temporary security on the top-up loan. The responsibility of repaying the loan still rests with you, the buyer.

A similar scheme requires the parents to re-mortgage or take out a second mortgage to pay for the shortfall of their offspring's negative equity.

If you are in a negative equity position, make an appointment to discuss your plans with your lender. You will probably get a more sympathetic ear if you have a good reason for moving and a good repayment track record.

The deposit

Sometimes, the estate agent will ask you for a small deposit when you make an offer. This indicates to the seller that you're making a serious offer. You do not necessarily have to oblige, but it is returnable should the sale fall through because of abnormalities arising from the conveyancing or surveys.

Allow about £100 for the estate agent deposit.

The main deposit forms part of the payment for the property and is paid to the seller via his solicitor or licensed conveyancer. It isn't paid until the exchange of contracts. Once you have exchanged contracts the purchase is legally binding, for both parties, and the deposit cannot normally be reclaimed. If you do not have enough ready money for the deposit you may need to arrange a bridging loan until you receive the mortgage or money from the sale of your property.

Allow between 5 and 10 per cent of the purchase price for the deposit.

Stamp Duty

Stamp Duty is a tax paid to the Government on the purchase of properties

---

Reducing Stamp Duty

If the purchase price you are offering includes fixtures and fittings, try to negotiate a lower price and settle up for the fixtures and fittings separately. The amount you have to pay Stamp Duty on is then lower; and if the purchase price is just over £60,000 you may be able to avoid Stamp Duty altogether.

Use your solicitor or licensed conveyancer to check that this is carried out legally. The value of the fixtures and fittings must be accurate, as it is fraudulent to avoid the Stamp Duty by making up items or inflating prices.

over £60,000. The duty is 1 per cent of the total purchase price. For example, if the house or flat costs £60,000 or under, no duty is paid, but if it costs between £60,001 and £60,100, duty is paid at 1 per cent, ie £601.

Legal costs, searches and surveys

The legal aspects of a move are carried out by a solicitor or licensed conveyancer. You will have to pay their professional fees and also the costs they incur on your behalf in the process. The conveyancing market is quite competitive because there are both solicitors and licensed conveyancers so shop around, getting three or four quotes. (For further details on licensed conveyancers and solicitors *see* Chapter 3, Using the Professionals.) You should expect to pay less than 1 per cent of the purchase price but it will depend upon the property and the area you are looking in. Fees can vary between £250 and £400 (plus VAT).

How much does the Land Registry cost?

Property Value (£)*	fee(£)
30,001 - 40,000	60
40,001 - 50,000	80
50,001 - 60,000	100
60,001 - 70,000	120
70,001 - 80,000	140
80,001 - 90,000	170
90,001 - 100,000	200
100,001 - 150,000	230
150,001 - 200,000	260
200,001 - 250,000	300

*Calculate from the value of the house given by the mortgage lender's valuation or price actually paid, rather than from the asking price.

Land Registry fee The Land Registry records all purchases of land or property in England or Wales and the change of ownership. The registered title to any particular piece of land describes it verbally and makes reference to the title plan. It includes the names of the owner and some mortgage details, rights over another person's land and any rights anyone else has over the land in the title. Your solicitor or licensed conveyancer will inspect the office copy of the register and the title plan from the Land Registry. The Land Registry charges a fee of £5 for each item inspected. If copies of other documents have to be obtained from the Registry, then further fees will be charged. A Land Registry fee is paid when the details are changed, i.e. you buy the property (see table above).

Not all properties are registered as yet. If you are buying an unregistered property, then it will need to be registered by your solicitor or licensed conveyancer within two months of the purchase. The deeds will be held by your lender until the mortgage is paid off.

Searches Your solicitor or licensed conveyancer checks with the local authority and other bodies for proposed developments that may affect the property, for example, plans for a new rail link, road widening or trunk roads.

Local authority searches show details relating only to the property itself and not to any nearby buildings. If the property is next to a vacant or derelict property, or open land, ask your solicitor or licensed conveyancer to check for any proposed developments.

The local authority is the main source of information but other searches can be carried out, for example with water companies, local mining companies and any prospective local developers.

If your solicitor or licensed conveyancer is local he should know the area and the most appropriate searches to carry out, but it is worth checking whether these are automatically included.

Problems associated with contaminated land have become more apparent recently. According to the Building Research Establishment it has been estimated that up to 50 per cent of new houses have been erected on contaminated land. This can have an effect on the materials of the building in the future due to aggressive chemicals, gases such as methane and unstable ground. It may be worth discussing this with your solicitor or licensed conveyancer, particularly if you are looking at new properties in the West Midlands area. Also consider Radon gas.

Allow around £60 to £90 for the local authority fee and about another £60 for additional searches.

Structural surveys
Home Buyer's Survey and Valuation This is a basic structural survey and should be considered as the minimum survey to have for any house purchase. Budget for £100 to £250.

Building structural survey This digs a bit deeper and looks at more important aspects such as the condition of the roof and floor. It may need specialists to examine particular points, such as wiring or the condition of any timber. Price depends very much on the size, age and condition of the property. It's worth paying a bit extra for this thorough survey because it could save you a lot of money in the long run.

There are no set fees for a surveyor's report, as it depends upon the property and the surveyor. Before employing a surveyor, negotiate the price so that both parties know what is involved and the costs. Budget for £200.

For further details about surveys *see* Chapter 3, Using the Professionals.

Remember You may need to budget for more than one set of searches and surveys if your first house choice falls through.

Lender's legal fees You will probably have to pay some legal fees on behalf of your lender. Usually you can use the same solicitor or licensed conveyancer, combining and saving on the costs.

Valuation report The lender has a valuation carried out on the property you are proposing to purchase to determine its true market value.

This is the maximum value of the mortgage the lender will offer you. If the purchase price is higher you may need to renegotiate with the seller or find the additional money yourself.

The value of the property is the security for the mortgage. The lender needs to be sure that, if for any reason the mortgage cannot be paid off, he can reclaim the full value of the mortgage by selling the house.

A simple valuation costs between £70 and £150, but not all lenders pass this cost on to you; for instance, Cheltenham & Gloucester Building Society don't. To save money most lenders will accept the valuation from the Home Buyer's Survey and Valuation.

Remember The valuation report is not a structural survey; it should not be relied upon to show any defects in the property, but it can be carried out at the same time to reduce costs.

Mortgage fees

Mortgage indemnity insurance This is a single premium paid if you arrange a mortgage for over 70 to 80 per cent of the lender's valuation. It is also sometimes called indemnity guarantee (MIG) premium, or mortgage indemnity premium. The premium is an insurance taken out by the lender to protect him in case the borrower defaults on payments, in which case the lender will sell the property to reclaim the loan. If the value of the house has decreased, the indemnity ensures that the lender can reclaim his finance. It is to protect the mortgage lender, not the buyer. The cost may be added to your mortgage or paid separately, sometimes up front, depending on your lender.

The cost of mortgage indemnity insurance varies depending upon what percentage mortgage you apply for and the lender you use. For example, a 90 per cent mortgage on a £60,000 property will vary from £300 to £960, while for a 100 per cent mortgage you could be paying anything up to £1,875.

Remember If you are comparing mortgage quotes, take into account the cost of the mortgage indemnity and when you will need to pay it.

Mortgage arrangements fees Depending upon the type of mortgage you are considering you may have to pay an arrangement fee. Costs vary but you should budget for around £250.

For further details on choosing a mortgage *see* Chapter 4, Arranging a Mortgage.

House-hunting

How much you have to spend while looking for a house will vary considerably, depending upon your circumstances.

You do not need to pay anything to an estate agent for the details or help he offers, as he is working for, and is paid by the seller.

Good Investment

If you have a young family it may be a good investment to pay for a child minder so you have fewer distractions while looking at properties.

If you are looking for a house in an unknown area, budget for travelling there to assess the area and to discover which districts are suitable, and to view potential properties.

You will also be making extra phone calls, and if you're travelling a distance you may need overnight accommodation and/or meals.

Home search relocation agencies If visiting the area in which you are contemplating purchasing a house is not practical, you could call upon the services of a relocation agency. Costs vary but are generally about $1\frac{1}{4}$ per cent of the purchase price, though some agencies charge a fixed price. For more about relocation agencies, *see* Chapter 3, Using the Professionals.

Removals

Unless you are not moving far and are considering doing it yourself, budget for hiring a removals firm.

A basic cost for a local move of a three-bedroom house is anything from around £300. However, costs will vary considerably from company to company, and will depend upon the circumstances of your move. You may need to allocate some money for storage.

If you are planning to do the move yourself, bear in mind the cost of hiring a suitable vehicle and providing food and drink for any extra pairs of hands you engage to help you.

A 3.5 tonne/$3\frac{1}{2}$ ton van costs around £65-£75 for a day. You may need it for longer if you have a lot of possessions or are moving some distance.

You may also need to pay for reconnection of the telephone line, a plumber to disconnect and reconnect a washing machine and dishwasher, or someone to fit the carpets at your new home.

You can make arrangements to have your mail redirected by the Post Office. Charges start at £6 for one month redirection.

For more about removals, see Chapter 8, Moving Home.

You can make arrangements to have your mail redirected by the Post

Office. Charges start at £6 for one month's redirection.

For more about removals, *see* Chapter 8, Moving Home.

CHECKLIST OF COSTS	
Calculating the cost of buying a house	
Deposit (10%)	
Stamp Duty (1%)	
Legal costs	
Land Registry	
Searches:	
Local authority	
Other	
Surveys*:	
Valuation Report	
Home buyer's Survey and Valuation	
Building Structural Survey	
Lender's legal fees	
Mortgage indemnity insurance	
Mortgage arrangement fee	
House-hunting	
Removals:	
Storage	
Hire of remover	
Post redirection	
Other	
Total	
* You will only need to pay for one or two of these.	

BUYING AND SELLING

The diagram below shows a simplified example of the most common process of buying and selling a house. The seller puts his house on the market first and waits for a secure buyer before buying a property for himself.

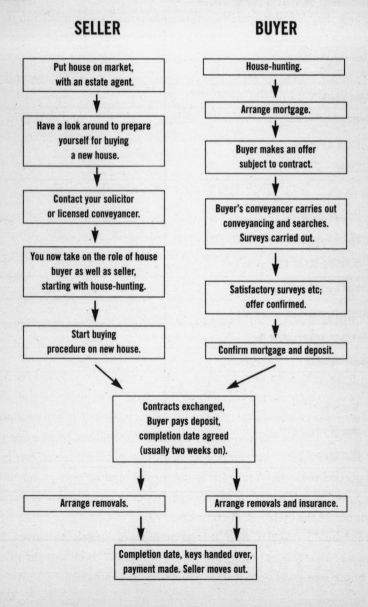

The aim is to organise the process so that the seller moves into his new house when the buyer moves into his.

Exceptions to this process include:

- where there is no property to sell (first-time buyers or when moving from rented accommodation)
- where the seller is prepared to move into rented accommodation in order to secure a sale even though he has not yet purchased a new property
- if you are opting for building your own new house (*see* Chapter 6, Having a Self-build House)
- buying or selling in Scotland (*see* Chapter 5, Buying and Selling in Scotland)

THE BUYING PROCESS

Once you have found your 'dream home' the serious stage of buying begins. As a guide, the time between putting in your offer and actual completion is around 12 to 16 weeks, but this will vary depending upon the circumstances.

Making an offer

If you haven't already lined up a solicitor or licensed conveyancer, now is the time to do so (*see* Chapter 3, Using the Professionals).

Put in your offer direct to the seller if they are selling privately, otherwise to their estate agent. When the market is slow, buyers can often afford to put in a lower offer than the asking price and negotiate a good deal. The seller may take some time to accept the offer. Once he has you can ask him not to take offers from any other potential buyer, but he is not obliged to do so. Your offer is not legally binding on you, nor is his acceptance of it binding on the seller; either can choose to pull out at any point before the exchange of contracts.

You should make it clear that your offer is 'subject to survey and contract'. Your solicitor or licensed conveyancer will check that the title of the house is in good order before you exchange contracts.

Let the seller or estate agent know your circumstances. Holding a mortgage certificate indicates to the seller that you are organised and prepared for buying.

The seller will ask for details of your solicitor or licensed conveyancer for their solicitor to contact to discuss the offer and other arrangements.

Putting your home on the market

Most movers try to secure the sale of their old home before looking for a new one. If you haven't started to sell your house yet, you're advised to do so as quickly as possible.

Arranging finance

If you have already discussed a mortgage, your lender will need to know about the property you are looking at and arrange a valuation report. Don't forget that if you are having a structural survey, the valuation can be combined to save you money.

Exchange of contracts

Once both the buyer and seller are happy with all the details stated in the contract and your conveyancer can confirm that there are no outstanding legal queries, the conveyancers exchange signed contracts. The sale is now

---

Gazumping and Gazundering

Gazumping is more common in a competitive market where there are a lot of buyers around. The seller accepts a higher offer from a third party between accepting an offer subject to contract and exchanging contracts. Sometimes you can enter into a 'lock-out' agreement where the seller agrees not to sell to anyone else as long as the contracts are exchanged within a certain time.

Gazundering is the opposite of gazumping and can occur in a slow buyers' market. Just before exchanging contracts the buyer reduces their offer, knowing that the seller is keen to sell and will probably accept the lower price rather than lose the sale.

Buying with a Friend

Cohabiting couples often don't have the same rights as married couples. There is in fact no such thing as a common-law husband or wife. You should therefore consider your rights if you are setting up home together. It may be all dreams and happiness now but it is worth sparing a thought and making arrangements in case something should go wrong in the future as you could well be liable for the whole of a joint mortgage should your partner disappear from the scene or their financial circumstances worsen.

Drawing up and signing a Cohabitation Contract prior to purchase will put in writing how ownership of the property is shared and what happens to your home and loan if you split up or if one of you dies. Verbal agreements can be difficult to stand by in years to come; promises can conveniently be forgotten.

The Cohabitation Contract can include any conditions you wish and is drawn up by your solicitor. There are standard forms for cohabitation agreements which can include financial arrangements stating who pays the mortgage, who can call for a sale, mutual wills, and who pays for and owns possessions.

Justice have a leaflet 'Living Together - Spell Out Your Rights' which is available from your local Citizens' Advice Bureau or solicitor.

legally binding for both parties. You must pay the deposit and arrange the completion date. Arrange buildings and contents insurance to run from the date contracts are exchanged as you are now liable for the property.

Remember If you are using money from selling one house to buy another, the dates you set for exchanging contracts and paying a deposit should allow time for cheques to clear through the banks.

Completion

This is the final day of the sale. After paying the outstanding balance, you are entitled to vacant possession of the property and will receive the keys.

OTHER WAYS OF BUYING PROPERTY

Buying by auction

A small proportion of properties are sold by auction. Usually it is in circumstances where the best market price is sought, for example if the property is unusual or individual and therefore difficult to put a price on, or if the house is being sold on behalf of other people. (Repossessed properties or properties being sold for executors come into this category.) This is an opportunity to pick up an unusual property, or a good bargain.

Estate agents will tell you if they have any suitable properties going to auction. If not, look out for properties displaying 'for sale by auction' boards or advertised in local papers.

Large London auctioneers often carry out group auctions for selling repossessed properties. If you are not fussed where you live, there will be properties all over the country available.

The *Estates Gazette* magazine is a good source of information, but you will probably have to order it from a newsagent.

Remember If you fail to buy the house, you lose all the money you have invested in conveyancing and other fees.

Preparing for an auction Because the auction is the final step of the sale, you should have any conveyancing carried out and your mortgage arranged. You will probably need to sell your old home. With this in mind it is a quick way of finding a property if you need to move promptly, but your choice of property may be limited or need work on it.

- Ask for the package compiled by the auctioneer. It will include full details of the property and the Memorandum of Agreement, which is equivalent to the contract.
- View the house.
- Organise a conveyancer (*see* Chapter 3, Using the Professionals) and instruct him or her to carry out searches and arrange surveys.
- If you like the property, set yourself a price limit to bid to, and arrange a mortgage.

> ### Buying Before the Auction
>
> If the sales details quote 'unless previously sold' the seller may be prepared to accept offers before the auction, but he will still expect a fast sale and you will be signing an auction contract. You will need to rapidly arrange conveyancing and finance.

Remember If you are buying at an auction you must realise that the fall of the hammer on your bid is equivalent to the exchange of contract as for a private sale. You have made a legal agreement and will be expected to pay a 10 per cent deposit there and then, with the remainder of the payment usually within 28 days.

At the auction If you are doubtful about your bidding ability you could appoint someone else to bid for you, but professionals such as solicitors will charge for their services.

The seller may be selling subject to a reserve price. If this is the case, it is normally stated in the particulars. The actual figure is not usually disclosed but if the auctioneer states something like 'I am going to sell this property today' it is an indication that the reserve price has been reached. If the reserve price is not reached the property will be withdrawn. If you were one of the final bidders you could approach the seller afterwards with the possibility of arranging a private sale.

Sale by tender

As an alternative to auction, sale by tender is like a blind auction; you don't know what the other potential buyers are offering. A Form of Tender is included in the sales details and sometimes sets out the contract details. Always check these details with your conveyancer, because often you can't pull out after the offer is accepted.

Buyers put their offers into an envelope, sometimes with a 10 per cent deposit. These must be received by the seller's agent by a specified date, at which time the seller will accept one of the offers.

Sale by tender is sometimes used when there have been two or three offers at similar prices.

CHAPTER 2

House-hunting

CONSIDERING WHERE TO BUY A HOUSE

Where you choose to buy your new house or flat may depend upon existing or predetermined factors but if you are starting afresh or are a first-time buyer, there are likely to be advantages and disadvantages with any location you're considering. Your circumstances and likes and dislikes will be the main influences on your decision, but here are some general points to think about, especially if you are changing your lifestyle through retirement or bringing up a family.

Built-up areas
Pros
- Close community for a growing family.
- Local services - schools, doctor, sports facilities - and other children close at hand.
- Greater variety of house size, price and age. More facilities for the old such as sheltered houses or developments designed for the less mobile. Suitable community and social services are more likely to be available.
- Local public transport and neighbours to share travelling with.
- Shops within walking distance which may be cheaper because of greater demand and stock a greater selection of goods than rural ones.
Cons
- Houses closer together so less privacy, smaller gardens, less playing space for children.
- More local activity: more street noise, pollution from traffic and possible late-night noise if you are near pubs or clubs.
- Street parking, if you don't have a garage or drive.
- Insurance for your home and car is often more expensive .
- Different schooling environment from village schools.

Rural areas
Pros
- More detached housing with land.
- Larger gardens: greater space for children to play or for growing your own fruit and vegetables.
- Land adjacent to the house may provide a potential for extensions, such as a larger garage, a conservatory or more living space.
- Greater privacy in the house and garden; less chance of being overlooked.
- Access to open spaces for leisure and often more peaceful surroundings.
- Cleaner air (but don't forget you may need to tolerate country activities such as the smell and noise from farming).
- Insurance premiums are often lower.

Cons
- A degree of isolation: possibly no immediate neighbours, so there's no one at hand in case of emergencies or to keep an eye on the place when you're away.
- A particular size house may come with more land than you really want. Large gardens need a lot of maintenance: mowing lawns, stocking with plants, weeding, trimming hedges.
- Services may be limited: some rural areas don't have mains gas, so you may need to adapt to Calor gas, or electric.
- Possibility of no main sewer: cesspools need regular emptying (recommended every 45 days) while septic tanks should be emptied about once a year. Both will cost you about £40 each time.
- Variety of house prices: depending upon quality and age of houses and locality to main centres. The village you like the look of may turn out to be in an expensive commuter belt.
- Country pursuits that can shatter the silence: watch out for scramble tracks or clay pigeon shooting.
- Transport considerations: you may need an extra car, as public transport in rural districts may be limited or non-existent.
- Small local shops or post offices with limited choice, and possibly higher prices.

Regional Variations in Cost

Council Tax is based on the council valuation and size of a property, but varies from district to district.

Services such as gas and electricity are charged differently by the privatised regional companies. Water charges, which are calculated either as water rates or by metering, vary in cost depending upon the water company.

- Limited local education: no secondary school nearby, fewer pre-school groups and possibly less companionship for children; library may only be a mobile library.
- The doctor or dentist may be in the next town.
- Limited or non-existent leisure facilities.
- Small rural communities are less inclined to have social facilities and you may find it difficult to integrate with 'the locals'.
- Larger phone bills to keep in touch with suburban friends, and travel costs for visiting – they may not want to trek out to see you so often!

Of course the idea of isolation, greater space and fewer people around are the very reasons some choose to move into rural areas.

TYPES OF PROPERTY

Moving into a larger house

You're likely to encounter many extra costs if you are considering expanding into a larger property. These include:

- Larger carpets
- More furniture
- Larger garden to tend: extra tools, and plants, professional help to maintain trees and possibly garden, and larger water bill if metering is in force
- Bigger bills for heating costs, water, Council Tax
- More decorating: more windows to curtain, larger/more rooms to

paper or paint, more cleaning (you may need to hire help)

- If you are moving from a flat, instead of a maintenance payment, you will have to maintain more yourself, such as the roof and property borders, fences or walls.
- Building insurance is often looked after by the leaseholder with a flat, but you will now have building and contents insurance on a larger property and probably on more belongings.

MOVING INTO A FLAT

There are some points to remember if you are contemplating moving into a flat, particularly if you haven't had one before.

Maintenance charge The cost of maintenance for common areas is shared between the residents and paid as a service or maintenance charge. If you are considering a basement, roof flat, or one with individual features such as a balcony, check that special maintenance for these is still shared by all the residents.

Your survey should show what improvements have been carried out recently and if any more are likely to be needed. Remember to have a survey encompassing the whole property not just your flat.

Shared facilities It's worth clarifying the aspect of shared areas and payments. Do you have any say in the work? Who cleans common areas? Have the service charge payments been paid without trouble by all the other residents in the past?

Also check the facilities such as the heating and water systems. Are they shared? How flexible are they?

Check any restriction stated in the lease, what activities are allowed, and how car parking is allocated. Are pets allowed?

Most of these should be included in the lease, but get your solicitor or licensed conveyancer to check it out thoroughly.

Living in the flat With flats, a decent-sized garden is often lacking and, if there is one, it may only be accessible to ground-floor flats. Check if it is communal.

You might miss the storage you had in the garage or shed.

Pets are not always welcome in flats.

External access can be limited depending upon the position of the flat. Where will the dustbin go? Are the lifts or stairs convenient?

You will probably have to be tolerant of neighbours, as you may be disturbed by their movements, particularly above.

Also consider how your activities will affect other flat dwellers - they may not appreciate your drum practice!

Will you have room for all the furniture you want? If the move is a temporary one, consider putting some belongings into store.

Insurance Insurance for the overall property is usually the responsibility of the landlord or management company. Check what this covers and make sure you are named as an occupant on the policy. You will still need your own contents insurance.

VIEWING POTENTIAL PROPERTIES

Before you start house-hunting, draw up a list of all the characteristics you will need from your new home, such as the number of bedrooms, the size of the kitchen, garage and study, and the size of the garden.

Take the estate agent's details with you so that you can check any points that may not be included or fully explained. (For details of the abbreviations used to describe properties, *see* DIY Selling, page 106.)

You may love, or hate, the appearance of a house, but it may have something to do with the current owner's possessions, so try and imagine the house with your furniture, children's toys, etc.

It's a good idea to take a tape measure to note down measurements. Will your furniture actually fit in the house?

Assessing location

It's difficult to judge the location of a property until you actually visit. Pay particular attention to the actual site: is it in a busy road (maybe a commuter short cut or main access road to a motorway)? Are there traffic lights, sharp bends or major junctions close by? Will car headlamps shine into your windows at night? Will you be disturbed by any other sources of noise, such as a nearby motorway, railway line or flight path? Are you opposite a light industrial estate? Is access to the property suitable? Do you share a drive or will there be enough street parking?

It's also important to make an assessment of the neighbours, especially if the property is semi-detached, a flat or located in a terrace; are their properties well-tended, for example?

If you are interested in the property, arrange a second visit at a different time of the week, say at a weekend or on a weekday evening.

Assessing the building

Any house buyer is advised to have at least a Home Buyer's Survey and Valuation (*see* Structural Surveys, page 13), but there are a few main structural points you could look out for when you're viewing a property:

- Which way does the property face? Are there likely to be any exposed damp walls that never see the sun?
- Check the exterior – can you see any flaking brickwork, crumbling pointing or cracks?
- Look for a damp-proof course – normally about 15cm (6in) from the ground. If it has been breached by items such as a concrete path or soil up close to the wall, watch out for signs of damp.
- Look out for damp inside too. Marks on the ceiling and walls could indicate a leaking roof, broken rainwater pipe or perished pointing.

The Effect of the Weather

Most houses look their best when it's warm and sunny, so bear this in mind if you are house-hunting in the summer. If you like the look of a property on a cold, wet, winter's day, there's a good chance you won't be making a rash choice.

Also, in the cold weather the heating will probably be on, so you can judge for yourself how efficient it is.

Tide marks and patches above the skirting boards may indicate rising damp. Discoloured walls may also indicate condensation due to poor ventilation.

- Ask about any treatments that may have been used, such as timber treatments (wood preservation wasn't standard until the early 1970s). If they are recent ask if there are guarantees for the work, and the name of the company.
- Cracks in the main walls, a bent chimney stack or doors that stick and don't have level door frames may be signs of subsidence.
- If the house is under ten years old, is it covered by any building guarantees such as the Buildmark or New Home Guarantee (*see* Building Guarantees, page 101-2) If so, make sure you obtain the handbook for the property if you do purchase it.

Tell your surveyor about any points you don't like the look of so that he or she can pay particular attention to them during the survey.

LEASEHOLD PROPERTIES

Unlike a freehold property, in which the building and the land it stands on are owned outright by the owner, leasehold property stands on land owned by someone else - the leaseholder or landlord. Any change of use or alterations need the approval of the leaseholder.

A lease usually runs for 100 years. Lenders require a lease to run for at least 20 years after the mortgage has been completed. When the lease expires, the ownership of the property reverts to the landowner.

Houses may be leasehold or freehold, but flats are nearly always leasehold.

Leasehold houses
Leasehold houses are more common in the north of England and south Wales. Who owns the leases depends on the area of the country; private estates often own leases for whole settlements. The owner of the property pays an annual ground rent.

Leasehold flats

The lease for a flat should include adequate provision for maintenance and repair of common parts of the building. A service or maintenance charge is payable, to cover the upkeep of the building and grounds. The leaseholder is responsible for maintaining property borders.

Enfranchisement

This means buying the lease to a property. Ever since the Government introduced the Leasehold Reform Housing and Urban Development Act in 1993, occupiers of leasehold properties have been able to apply to buy the freehold at a fair price. You must have lived in the property for the previous three years. As the occupier, you serve a notice on the landlord stating your intention to buy, before the lease expires. The landlord has to have a very good reason to refuse to sell the lease. It can be a long, drawn-out process, particularly if it is the leasehold for a block of flats. Buying a freehold will save on ground rent or service charges but as with buying any property you will need to employ a conveyancer, and pay the landlord's legal bills and other costs such as Stamp Duty and Land Registration.

Houses For further information refer to 'Leasehold Houses – Your right to buy the freehold of your house or extend your lease' by the Department of Environment and available from Citizens' Advice Bureaux.

Flats The occupiers of a group of flats can jointly buy the freehold as long as two thirds of the residents support the idea. Before serving the initial notice on your landlord, a lot of preparation work is involved, such as forming a committee, setting up a joint fund to cover initial expenses and deciding upon the management arrangements. Freeholders may also wish to employ a management firm to organise the servicing of the flats.

Further details are available in the leaflet 'Leasehold Flats – Your right to buy the freehold of your building or renew your lease' (details as above).

Remember Scotland has a different system of land ownership (*see* Chapter 5, Buying and Selling in Scotland).

BUYING AN OLD HOUSE

Old properties often have great appeal, with individual character and a solid, mature appearance. But old does not necessarily mean well built and sound. There are a few points to be considered, especially if the property has not been maintained to cater for modern standards of living.

Potential for improvement

If the house you are looking at is the one for you 'as long as we can change this or put an extension there', then bear in mind the feasibility of your ideas.

Consider whether your proposed alterations will be in keeping with the age and style of the house, and neighbouring houses, particularly in a terrace. A classic mistake includes replacement windows and doors with modern, unsympathetic styling.

If appropriate, you could consider contacting The Victorian Society or The Georgian Group for advice on preserving your house. Both offer advisory leaflets to help you carry out appropriate restoration.

It's often a good idea to employ a qualified architect or surveyor to plan and oversee any alterations you are considering. For local contractors

---

Interested in purchasing and renovating a historic building?

Contact the Society for the Protection of Ancient Buildings. SPAB accept membership from people who are sympathetic to the conservation of old buildings and you must agree with the principles set out in the Manifesto. Annual membership costs £24 and gives you access to details of historic buildings in need of repair and for sale, as well as publications and courses specially for owners of old buildings. They can also offer advice on choosing an adviser or supplier of traditional materials. For further information, or a copy of the leaflet 'Look Before You Leap - Guidelines to buying an old building', contact SPAB.

For property in Scotland a list of historical or architecturally interesting buildings for sale is available from the Scottish Civic Trust (Buildings at risk service).

In Northern Ireland, contact Ulster Architectural Heritage Society.

contact the Royal Institute of British Architects or the Royal Institution of Chartered Surveyors.

Renovation grants may be available to you, but application for them or for planning permission may not necessarily be the quick simple answer.

Renovation grant This may be available from local authorities for properties needing immediate repairs or work to bring them up to modern standards. You can apply for one if your property is unfit or is in serious disrepair.

The provision of the grant by the authority depends upon the type of work necessary and your circumstances; you will be means-tested when you apply. The financial assessment, which will include other household members with an interest in the property, is similar to applying for housing benefit - your weekly income will be assessed, and family status considered. The amount of the grant will depend upon your income. Obviously, the higher your income the more you will be expected to pay, but if your income is low you could be eligible for a full or substantial grant.

Further details are available in a leaflet, 'House Renovation Grants', from the renovation grants department at your local authority or from the Citizens' Advice Bureau. Some areas have an Agency Service, a local centre which can provide advice and practical help on all aspects of repairs and improvements, including the renovation grants system.

Disabled facilities grant A grant may be available to adapt a property for a disabled person, for example improving access into and around the home and adapting existing essential facilities within it. These grants are mandatory, but a discretionary grant is available to make a property suitable for the accommodation, welfare or employment of a disabled person. A Department of the Environment leaflet, 'Help for Disabled People with Adaptation and Other Works', provides basic information, but grants are also covered in the 'House Renovation Grants' leaflet mentioned above.

Worth Waiting For?

If you don't think you will get a full renovation grant, consider the application realistically. If you are waiting around for the grant to be processed, the money you spend on somewhere to live in the meantime may be more than you get in the grant at the end.

Grants for a building of special interest If the house you are buying is listed or in a conservation area, you may be able to get a grant for repair or maintenance from some local authorities or from English Heritage. For further information, the leaflets 'Principles of Repair' and 'Repair Grants' are available from English Heritage. If you are buying a house in Wales or Scotland, contact Cadw (Heritage Wales) or Historic Scotland. If buying in Northern Ireland, details can be obtained from the Historic Monuments Department, Department of the Environment for Northern Ireland.

Remember If you think you might be eligible for a grant, you mustn't carry out any work until the property has been assessed and a grant offered otherwise your application may be refused. The local authority will ask for at least two quotes for the work. They may be able to send you details of suitable local contractors.

Planning permission Planning permission is obtained from your local planning authority. You may need it for any alterations or extensions, particularly if they change the look or external aspect of the building. Planning permission is also needed if you are intending to change the use of the property. A planning permission application for house alterations costs £80.

You are allowed to carry out some work without planning permission, so it's worth contacting the planning officer at the local authority to discuss what you are considering.

You should also ask about building regulations. These are concerned with the materials and methods of building adopted. Regulations for work

Do You Need Planning Permission?

You don't usually need it for:

- small house extensions such as conservatories, sun lounges, loft conversions, dormer windows and roof additions
- buildings and structures on land around your house, such as garages, garden sheds, greenhouses and swimming pools
- adding a porch, unless it will be larger than 3 sq m (3.6 sq yd), more than 3 m (10 ft) high or less than 2 m (6 ½ ft) from a road
- putting up fences and walls
- patios or hard standing for vehicles and driveways
- satellite dishes and television and radio aerials
- decoration, repair, maintenance and demolitions
- replacing windows
- putting in skylights or roof lights

Even if planning permission isn't needed you should consider whether or not you are affecting your neighbours' 'right to light'. If you will be overshadowing a window and it has been there 20 years or more, you could face legal action.

But planning permission is needed for:

- use of a caravan in your garden as a home for someone
- dividing off part of your house for business use
- work that may obstruct the view of road users
- work which involves new or wider access to a major road
- additions and extensions to a flat or maisonette

You'll also need it for some of the 'permitted development' examples above in certain circumstances. These include extensions that are less than 20 m (22 yd) from a public highway (i.e. roads, footpaths) and those that will be 15 per cent larger in volume than the existing property, or greater than 70 cu m (91.5 cu yd). Property that is listed or in a conservation area is subject to additional restrictions. For further details the Department of the Environment leaflet, 'Planning - a guide for householders', can be obtained free from the local planning authority.

Building Regulations are concerned with the standard of building materials and methods. For further information contact the Building Control Department at your local authority.

carried out in conservation areas are strict (see below). The Building Control Department at your local authority will be able to advise you about building regulations.

Most applications for planning permission are dealt with within eight weeks. Sorting out grants and having the building work done can take considerably longer, so bear this in mind before buying a property that needs work on it. You may not be able to live in the property for some time.

Buying a listed building

Buildings of architectural or historical interest are listed by the Secretary of State for National Heritage following consultation with English Heritage, to protect them against inappropriate alteration. In Wales, buildings are listed by the Secretary of State for Wales in consultation with Cadw (Heritage Wales); in Scotland, they are listed by the Secretary of State for Scotland, in consultation with Historic Scotland. There are about 500,000 listed buildings in England which have legal protection. You are likely to need listed building consent, for any work, inside or out, that will affect the character of the building, in addition to any planning permission also needed. The conservation officer in the local planning department can provide more information on restrictions.

Buildings in conservation areas

Local authorities can designate areas of special architectural or historical interest as conservation areas. Conservation areas are protected to ensure that their character or interest is retained. Whole towns or villages may be conservation areas, or simply one particular street.

Stricter regulations are laid down for conservation areas. Protection includes all buildings and all types of trees that are larger than 7 cm across at 1.5 m above the ground. There may be limitations for putting up signs, outbuildings or items such as satellite dishes. Any developments in the area will probably have to meet strict criteria, such as using traditional or local materials.

This also applies to property in national parks, designated Areas of Outstanding Natural Beauty and the Norfolk and Suffolk Broads.

Whether or not a property is listed or is deemed to be in a conservation area will show up when your conveyancer carries out the local authority search.

There are grants available from the local authority for structural repairs to listed buildings. English Heritage may also be able to help with the costs if the building is of outstanding interest. (*See* Grants for a building of special interest, page 33-4.)

BUYING A NEW HOUSE

There are many benefits to buying a newly built house. From the practical point of purchasing you will not be in a buying–selling chain. But you may be restricted by the completion date of the building, especially if the construction takes longer than expected, so keep in touch with the builder to check progress.

Features to look for
You have the advantage of being the first occupants. Sometimes you can ask for particular fixtures and fittings and colour schemes - you don't need to endure someone else's tasteless wallpaper until you can afford to redecorate. Nor should there be any need for maintenance or major DIY jobs.

Advantages you should expect with a newly built house:
- Ample sockets in convenient places.
- Most new houses have fitted kitchens.
- Conservatories are also becoming a standard feature of new houses.
- Maximum insulation, and energy-efficient heating and water systems.

A new house today uses 50 per cent less energy than a house built 15 years ago; consider the savings over an older property. An energy rating indicates how energy-efficient a house is. The National House-Building Council uses a rating scheme based on the National Energy Services scheme, in which houses are given a rating between 0 and 10. A house rated 10 will be very energy efficient and have very low running costs for

The 'Secured by Design' Scheme

This covers some new home developments. The houses displaying the logo shown here meet safety and security requirements set by a number of police forces to deter against crime and prevent fire its size. Not all new houses will display a rating but it may be worth asking the developer.

Security and safety are built in to new houses: smoke alarms are standard and security locks on doors and windows may also be included. New estates of houses usually have proper street lighting.

When the housing market is slow, developers may offer incentives to buyers, particularly if they are trying to sell the last few properties. It's worth shopping around but do consider what the extras are worth. Fitted carpets throughout may seem an added bonus, but check the quality – are they going to wear out in next to no time?

Many developers also offer part exchange, which is an asset if you are having difficulty selling your old property. But you may have to accept a lower price for your house or some other restriction such as a limit on the price of house they will offer you.

Remember a property developer who buys up older houses in part exchange may have houses for sale, other than the new developments, from previous exchanges.

Finding a new house

Contact local developers to see if they have any developments underway or planned in the area in which you are looking. Property magazines such as *Nationwide Properties*, *House Buyer and Mortgage Finder*, *What House?* and *Home Finder* or *What Mortgage?* also advertise details from developers. These are available from newsagents.

You can even house-hunt from the comfort of your own home. 'New Homes' is available on ITV Teletext, page 370. Set up by the New Homes Marketing Board, it gives details of the advantages of new houses and adverts for developments in your area. 'Property Plus' on Channel 4, page 544, provides information on buying a house, including mortgage details.

Remember this is also an advertising service and does not cover the whole market. You should still shop around for other details and offers.

The National House-Building Council (NHBC) is the largest body overseeing the industry. Standards are set to which NHBC builders must conform. About 90 per cent of new housing is built by NHBC members and awarded the Buildmark warranty. For particular developments you may find builders displaying a Pride in the Job award. This is presented, by the NHBC, to the best 100 site supervisors. It gives buyers a benchmark when considering quality, with the knowledge that houses have been built to a high standard. Contact the NHBC for details of award-winning developments.

The ultimate in buying a new house is having one built to your requirements – *see* Chapter 6, Having a Self-build House.

Building guarantees
All new houses should be built to certain standards and qualify for one of the building industry guarantees. These building guarantees are normally essential for you to obtain a mortgage and they also make the property attractive to purchasers when you come to move.

Types of construction
New homes may be of a timber-framed construction or brick and block. For further details *see* Chapter 6, Having a Self-build House.

BUYING A RENTED HOUSE

Right-to-buy scheme
If you rent your house from your council, a new town, a housing association (non-charitable) or a housing action trust, you will probably be able to buy it from them, at a discounted price.

In order to buy:
- You must have a secure tenancy
- You must have spent at least two years as a tenant of your current landlord or another right-to-buy landlord,
- The house or flat must be a separate dwelling that is your main or only home.

You are able to buy the house with a joint tenant or up to three other members of your family who live with you, as long as it has been their main home for at least one year. But consider whether you need an agreement to regulate matters (*see* Buying with a Friend, page 21).

Discounted price The saving you make in buying your house depends upon how long you have been a public sector tenant, known as your qualifying period. This can be accumulated for different properties and does not need to be continuous.

The minimum qualifying time is two years and starts off with a discount of 32 per cent for a house or 44 per cent for a flat off the market value. Subsequently the discount for a house is an extra 1 per cent for each year you've been a tenant, up to a maximum of 60 per cent for 30 years or more. For a flat you have an extra 2 per cent for each year, up to a maximum of 70 per cent for 15 years or more (see table on page 41).

If you sell your house within three years of purchase, you will have to pay back some of the discount.

Application Fill in an application form (RTB1) available from your landlord. You may also be able to arrange a mortgage from your landlord but more likely will need to approach a commercial lender such as a bank or building society (*see* Chapter 4, Arranging a Mortgage).

You will need to follow a buying procedure similar to that for buying a private home, such as using a conveyancer, paying a Land Registry fee, paying Stamp Duty. These details are covered in Costs of Moving, pages 11-17.

Remember If you buy your house there will be extra costs that you haven't normally paid:

Qualifying period (years)	Discount for a House (%)	Discount for a Flat (%)
2	32	44
5	35	50
10	40	60
15	45	70
20	50	70
25	55	70
30	60	70
over 30	60	70

- Council Tax (may have been included in your rent)
- Water rates (may have been included in your rent)
- Building insurance
- Service charges if you are buying a flat

Rent-to-mortgage scheme

If you can't afford to buy your property in one go, you can buy it with mortgage repayments. To start with, you pay a lump sum which is less than the right-to-buy price. You can borrow the money from a commercial lender and re-pay the same each month as you now pay in rent.

The scheme is available to public tenants. The qualification criteria and the discounts are similar to the right-to-buy scheme. It was introduced in October 1993 but so far has not had a very encouraging take-up rate.

More about the schemes

Further details about both schemes are available in a leaflet, 'Your right to buy your home', produced by the Department of the Environment and available from Citizens' Advice Bureaux and libraries.

Remember Although these schemes look attractive, you will still have to pay for other costs involved in house buying such as conveyancing and mortgage arrangement fees (*see* Costs of Moving, pages 11-17).

Shared ownership

There are properties made available on a shared-ownership basis especially for people who can't buy a house outright. The types of property are usually one-, two- or three-bedroom houses or flats, but availability and price vary according to location. A housing association or local housing authority provides and may manage the properties on shared-ownership terms. You can buy a share of the property, from 25 per cent to 75 per cent, and pay rent on the remainder. In the future you have the opportunity to buy a further share in the property and sometimes buy it outright at a later stage.

Even though you only own a part of the property you have the same rights and responsibilities of an owner-occupier. Repairs and decoration, inside and out, are your responsibility. Insurance for the structure is dealt with by the housing association but you will have to pay a service charge.

Entering a shared-ownership scheme involves all the procedures associated with buying a house (*see* Costs of Moving, pages 11-17).

Who can apply?   Shared ownership is often provided for first-time buyers and priority is given to local authority or housing association tenants and those on a waiting list.

Selling a shared-ownership property   You can either just sell the part of the property that you own or buy the remaining portion of the property and sell it as a whole. Some associations may restrict the sale price of a property to keep it available as low-cost housing.

The sale of some shared-ownership property is restricted, so that you cannot buy, and sell, the whole property outright. The housing association can buy back the property to ensure that it is available for future shared-ownership schemes.

Any restrictions relating to the property and the share that can be bought or sold should be detailed on the lease, and the housing association should inform you if this is the case before you buy.

Details of local housing associations are available from your local authority or by contacting one of the regional Housing Corporation offices (details can be found in Yellow Pages).

CHAPTER 3

Using the Professionals

You will be dealing with lots of people while buying and selling a house. The important point to keep in mind is that you are buying the services of professionals, so make sure that they know what you want, and that you know how, when and at what price you will get the service you require. Ask what fees will be charged, and if you are unsure about specific details always ask for clarification from the expert.

MONEY LENDERS

There are many institutions offering mortgages. Building societies and banks are the most common lenders.

What should you be offered?

There are various forms of mortgage (*see* Chapter 4, Arranging a Mortgage) and lenders should be willing to discuss all the options with you. Different companies may have more popular packages but don't be pressurised into signing immediately; shop around.

You will be asked to fill out a form to give the lender some indication of your income and normal monthly expenditure. From this they will be able to give you a mortgage certificate stating how much they are willing to offer (subject to property valuation and surveys). This is not a confirmed offer but it will indicate to a seller that you are a serious buyer and have already considered the finance.

Who can offer you a mortgage?

Building societies Still the largest providers of mortgages, building societies can also arrange investments for customers.

Banks A bank is often the first port of call if you already have accounts at a branch. All the high street banks offer a range of mortgages.

There is not much to choose between taking a mortgage with a building society or with a bank. Your decision will be influenced by the types of mortgage and the rates of interest offered.

Local authority If you are opting for a right-to-buy or rent-to-mortgage scheme, you will be able to take out a mortgage through the landlord, but you are not obliged to (*see* Chapter 2, House-hunting).

Housing associations Housing associations operating low-cost ownership through shared-ownership schemes may be able to help you arrange a mortgage, or may be able to recommend local mortgage lenders which they know to be helpful.

Insurance companies Life insurance is needed for endowment mortgages (see page 62). Insurance companies may also offer mortgages linked to their insurance policies.

Builders and property developers As an incentive to buy, builders or developers may offer to arrange your mortgage for you. They are often able to get good deals with low interest rates for the start of the mortgage, but rates may increase rapidly in the long term. Check that the developer is reputable.

Remember Estate agents are often owned by companies that offer mortgages such as banks and building societies. If they offer to arrange your mortgage, their broker will probably be tied to certain packages. So shop around to get an idea of other offers.

Independent financial advisors

Independent advisors do the work of finding a mortgage for you. They don't actually lend the money themselves, but find someone who will.

They provide a wide view of the mortgage market offering greater choice. Higher-risk mortgages will often have more stringent conditions. They may charge an arrangement fee.

Expect an advisor to offer a choice of mortgage schemes with written quotations, including the arrangement fee, if any, so that you can compare the offers critically.

It is recommended that you let your solicitor check over anything before you sign.

Remember Choose an independent financial advisor who is a member of the Independent Financial Advisors Association (IFAA). Lists of members are available from the IFAA.

CONVEYANCERS

Conveyancing is the legal process of buying a house and transferring its ownership.

Buying and selling a house in Scotland is a different affair. There are no licensed conveyancers and most property is sold through solicitors' offices. *See* Chapter 5, Buying and Selling in Scotland.

Choosing a conveyancer

You can use a licensed conveyancer or a solicitor. Both offer a house-buying service and carry out the legal work involved. The difference is that a licensed conveyancer is a specialist dealing with property law. There are fewer licensed conveyancers but their fees are similar to solicitors. If you choose a solicitor rather than a licensed conveyancer, ensure that his main work is property conveyancing.

Personal recommendation is a good way of finding out about solicitors or licensed conveyancers. Or, if you have already had successful dealings with a solicitor for other affairs, you could approach the firm to find a member who specialises in house purchases.

Your bank, building society or estate agent may be able to recommend a licensed conveyancer or solicitor. The Law Society's directory of solicitors, available at local libraries and Citizens' Advice Bureaux, will give you an idea of who is operating in your area. Similarly, details of licensed conveyancers are available from the Council for Licensed Conveyancers or Citizens' Advice Bureaux.

Always ask for a written estimate, covering all the costs, and the terms of agreement from a licensed conveyancer or solicitor before asking them to work for you. Discuss any points in their quotation you are not sure about and check that all your requirements are included.

A local licensed conveyancer or solicitor is preferable. When you first make contact with them, they will be able to comment on any local irregularities such as conservation areas or possible developments that they know of.

They will also be more familiar with local conditions such as the length of time the local authority searches normally take.

Remember You can use the same conveyancer for selling your house and buying a new one. However, you are not allowed to use the same conveyancer as the seller of the property you are trying to buy, or the person buying your house from you.

What to expect from your conveyancer

In this section the term conveyancer is used to mean either a licensed conveyancer or a solicitor carrying out conveyancing for you.

The main job of a conveyancer is to ensure that the property you are considering has a good title and there are no definable problems in the making.

Unlike consumer goods for which you have legal comeback if they are faulty or not fit for their purpose, there is no guarantee with a house (unless it has recently been built). Therefore, any pitfalls must be identified before you commit yourself to buy.

You should try to achieve a good balance of communication with your conveyancer. Provide him with as much information as you have, such as plans for extensions or alterations so that these can be taken into account from the start. The details will have to be relayed to the surveyor that you or the lender contact for the surveys.

The conveyancer will be working from the particulars provided by the estate agent, and is unlikely to see the actual property, so make him aware of any potential causes for concern that you detect when viewing. Ask him to make enquiries about anything happening on neighbouring properties, for example extensions that would cut out your light.

There will be periods where nothing seems to be happening. This may not necessarily be the fault of the conveyancer but due to other parties involved, such as the local authority. Be patient but keep in touch and ask for explanations of anything that is not clear during the course of the proceedings.

Conveyancers' main tasks: purchase

The conveyancer's job begins as soon as you have put in your offer (which is made subject to searches and surveys, and is not confirmed until they are completed).

Before confirming an offer

- Make local authority and other relevant searches.
- Check the seller's right to sell and that there are no complications such as sitting tenants, undisclosed mortgages, alterations that didn't have planning permission or disputes over boundaries and land ownership.
- Examine the details about the property at the Land Registry, or details about the history of the property going back at least 15 years if the house is unregistered.
- Find out about any shared driveways or drains, your right to access and any public right to access.
- Check boundaries and who is responsible for their upkeep.
- Check guarantees for any previous work such as damp treatment or building work.

- Sometimes arrange surveys and valuation report (*see* Chapter 2, House-hunting).

  If buying a newly built house:
- Check that the house is built correctly, that all services have been laid on, and that responsibility for maintenance of services such as drainage and sewerage has been handed over to the local authority.
- Check who has responsibility for the maintenance of access roads.
- Confirm any restrictions imposed by the developer, such as future alterations, cutting down of trees or parking restrictions.

Before contracts are exchanged

- Examine the draft contract, ensuring that all points are included, such as what fittings are included in the sale, and remedial work arranged by the seller prior to the exchanging of contracts.
- Exchange contracts with the seller's conveyancer (identical copies of the contract will have been signed by you and the seller).
- Receive deposit.
- Arrange signature of mortgage documentation before or after contracts have been exchanged.

After completion

- Notify the lender and insurance companies of the completion.
- Arrange payment of the Stamp Duty.
- Register you as the owner with the Land Registry along with details of your lender. He may require you as well as the seller to sign the Transfer document. Pass the deeds on to the lender.
- Send you a statement confirming that everything has been completed and any monies due to you.

Remember   You may also need to discuss with your conveyancer joint ownership; provision if one party should die or you become separated; any extras you are buying with the house that are, or are not, included in the particulars. A list clarifying the details should be included in the contract.

Conveyancers' main tasks: sale

- Liaise with the buyer's conveyancer in presenting any details about the property.
- Ensure that mortgages, and any other financial arrangements such as hire purchase, are cleared on completion.
- Draw up a draft contract and package including a copy of the title deeds or entry at the Land Registry. Deeds will need to be obtained from your lender.
- If the property is not registered with the Land Registry, details about the property, from the title deeds over at least the last 15 years, need to be prepared.
- Receive the deposit on behalf of the seller. If it is stated in the contract that the conveyancer is to act as 'agent for the vendor', the payment will be passed on for the seller to put towards his purchase.

TransAction Protocol

This is a scheme introduced by the Law Society to streamline the buying–selling process for England and Wales. The seller's solicitor decides whether or not to use it. If he does use it, then he will put together a pack of information that the buyer's solicitor needs. This includes the property registration details (or title deeds if the property is unregistered), a standard list of fixtures and fittings and details such as who is responsible for maintaining different property borders.

The Home Charter Scheme (Northern Ireland)

The Home Charter Scheme was set up for use by solicitors in Northern Ireland. It sets standards of service when solicitors help you buy or sell a property. The rules include using clear, simple and unambiguous language and giving regular reports on the progress of transactions.

When selecting a solicitor look for one who is registered as a Home Charter Solicitor.

Doing your own conveyancing

It is possible to carry out your own conveyancing if you have the time to spare and wish to reduce the costs of buying. Look out for books on conveyancing in your local library. They give details of all the procedures and whom to contact for searches and surveys.

DIY conveyancing is less common these days because the cost saving is not so great now that conveyancers are more competitive, and because it takes up a lot of your time. Also, as you almost certainly have to pay your lender's legal costs, it does not cost much more to have the same solicitor do the work for you and the lender at the same time.

ESTATE AGENTS

Buying a house or flat

When you start house-hunting contact several estate agents and visit their offices to discuss what you are looking for. Look out for agents advertising the sort of property you are looking for in their windows. They will give you details of current properties on the market and put you on their mailing list.

Do keep in contact with estate agents to reinforce your interest.

Selling a house or flat

Estate agents are employed by you as the seller, to advertise and find a buyer for your property as quickly as possible.

What to expect from your estate agent

- Advice on the selling price of the house – they will know the local market.
- Advice on the best way to sell and where to advertise; they should discuss an advertising budget with you.
- Some estate agents, including those that are members of the National Association of Estate Agents, have a computer listing which is available to other branches in the area, offering wider publicity.
- A meeting and visit to assess the value of the house and take down

details about it in order to put together the sales particulars. As a result of the Property Misdescriptions Act, estate agents have to avoid using ambiguous descriptions, such as a 'mature garden' when they mean 'overgrown'. If you are asked to check them, take a careful look at the points; these details give the first impression and could determine whether or not you go on the short list for a viewing.

- They may ask for details of recent bills, such as Council Tax and electricity costs. They should also be willing to give advice on which fixtures and fittings are best included in the sale.
- They should be willing to show potential buyers around your property if you are not available, or accept your wishes if you request to be around when any buyers visit.
- Don't expect to have to pay for a 'for sale' board, although some agents make a charge.

Remember The estate agent doesn't necessarily show you the particulars he has put together, so ask for a copy before they are printed if you want to check the text.

Choosing an estate agent to sell your home You may have had successful dealings in the past with an estate agent, which is sufficient proof for you to go back to the same one. Alternatively, you could accept recommendations from friends and family. Check around to see who is selling houses in your area and how many have 'Sold' on the board.

Bear in mind these points when comparing estate agents:

- They ought to sell your type of property or specialise in one particular area of the market.
- They should be a member of one of the professional bodies such as the National Association of Estate Agents, the Royal Institution of Chartered Surveyors, the Incorporated Society of Valuers and Auctioneers, the Architects' and Surveyors' Institute or the Association of Building Engineers. Members have to obey codes of conduct and participate in indemnity schemes to protect you.
- Obtain quotes of fees, including the basic charge and any extras you

---

Watch the Wording

Don't confuse 'sole agency' with 'sole selling rights'. An agent given 'sole selling rights' will claim commission even if he did not actually introduce the buyer. If you find the wording of the agent's contract unclear it would be advisable for your solicitor to check it for you.

---

might have to pay for, such as advertising in specialist publications.
• Choose at least two agents to value the house, before instructing an agent.

Remember The highest quoted valuation from an estate agent may encourage you to sell through them, but bear in mind that buyers will have a valuation to check the price. If the price was too high, you may have to accept a lower offer – that's if they are not discouraged in the first place by the high asking price.

Selling through one or more estate agents

Sole agency Offering an agent 'sole agency' may reduce the fee. Often sellers instruct an agent with sole agency for a limited period when they first put the house on the market. After this time you can instruct additional agents, or change agents completely. With sole agency, you still have the right to sell privately.

Joint sole agents With this arrangement, two or more agents co-operate in the house sale and split the commission. The agents may charge a higher commission than for sole agency but less than for multiple agency.

Multiple agency This means that you have several agents trying to sell your home, but only pay the agent which actually sells your property.

Remember Before agreeing to use an agent, check how much the withdrawal fee will be. It can be in the region of £100 if you change your selling arrangement. The fee is charged to cover the cost of advertising your home.

SURVEYORS

One or more surveyors are needed to carry out a valuation report on behalf of the lender and any structural building surveys needed. There are three types of survey: a valuation report, a basic structural survey known as a Home Buyer's Survey and Valuation, and a building structural survey (sometimes called a full structural survey). Your lender may instruct a valuation report but with prior arrangement will usually accept a valuation included with a structural survey (see Costs of Moving House, pages 11-17).

Choosing a surveyor

The largest professional association of surveyors is the Royal Institution of Chartered Surveyors (RICS). Members of the Incorporated Society of Valuers and Auctioneers (ISVA) also carry out home surveys. Members of both RICS and ISVA use standard procedures when carrying out a Home Buyer's Survey and Valuation.

If you are not sure who to approach, ask friends and relatives for recommendations or contact one of the associations above or the Architects' and Surveyors' Institute for details of members.

Surveyors will carry out a Home Buyer's Survey and Valuation or a building structural survey but may need to call in extra specialists to rectify particular problems such as timber protection or rising damp. You will have to pay extra for this on top of your surveyor's fee. When you arrange a survey, discuss exactly what you want and ask to be taken through the final report if you are unclear about any aspects.

Make it clear whether you want just the Home Buyer's Survey and Valuation, or a building structural survey.

Home Buyer's Survey and Valuation

An HBSV is a more detailed survey than a simple valuation report but is less extensive than a building structural survey. It is the least that should be considered to check the condition of a potential buy. It follows a standard format prepared by RICS and should be carried out by a RICS registered surveyor. Details that will be included are:

- the general condition of the property and external features such as woodwork, gutters and downpipes and damp-proof course
- any structural defects likely to affect materially the value of the property
- the true current value of the property in the open market
- the estimated reinstatement cost for insurance purposes, i.e. how much it would cost to rebuild the house if it should burn down

Lofts and cellar space are only inspected if they are reasonably accessible.

Building structural survey

Although more expensive, a full survey can be invaluable to ensure that there are no major structural faults that could prove expensive in the future. It will also tell you in detail about minor defects which, in the long run, you can't ignore.

The survey is more thorough and includes examining:

- the roof space, cellar and timbers
- under floors if coverings are easily removable
- services including drainage, wiring and central heating

You should ask permission of the occupier if you want to disturb any furniture or fixtures.

The inspection can take several hours to provide all the detail needed. It will report any problems with the physical parts of the building, including testing the walls for dampness and the timber for damage.

If there are any potential problems that you may have noticed when you viewed the property, such as cracks in the walls or stains that could indicate damp, draw them to the attention of your surveyor.

If you have any aspirations on changing the structure such as knocking down walls, building an extension or opening up fireplaces, ask your surveyor to consider the practicality of this.

If any remedial work is needed, your lender may retain some of the loan until work is carried out. You may want to negotiate a lower price with the seller to compensate or put in the contract that the work should be carried out at the seller's expense before completion. Always ask for a guarantee. If you need to carry out any work, get at least three quotes to give you an idea of the cost.

HOME SEARCH RELOCATION AGENTS

If you are moving to a distant region and regular visits to consider potential areas or properties are not practical, you can employ a relocation agent to carry out the initial house-hunting for you. They can take account of all the requirements you suggest, like proximity to schools, towns, shops and public transport. They will even negotiate the price for you. Once they have found a potential property you can then visit to see if it is suitable before an offer is made.

The Association of Relocation Agents produces a directory of agents which is free to house-buyers.

The cost of using a relocation agent is about $1^1/_4$ per cent of the purchase price. There may be a registration fee, but it does save you a lot of leg work.

CHAPTER 4

Arranging a Mortgage

Most people who want to buy a property need a mortgage – a loan to buy a home over a period of years, using the home as security for the loan. Getting a mortgage used to be quite simple. The source was usually a building society which offered a choice between a repayment mortgage and an endowment mortgage. A deposit was required, there were strict criteria set for borrowing, and the mortgage was set at a variable rate over a period of time that normally did not exceed the borrower's retirement age at the latest.

Nowadays things are very different. The choice of mortgage and payment schemes is so varied that a scheme can be tailor-made to suit individual circumstances. Deposits are not always required, and mortgages can be for up to 99 years – though this is very rare! Some mortgages have an investment or insurance element included in them, which can be more expensive and less flexible. It is essential, therefore, to make sure you know what you need and what you may be getting when you apply for a homeloan. Here are some basic tips to think about before you start looking.

Talking to mortgage lenders

Getting good mortgage advice should be easy, but isn't so, necessarily. As soon as you know that you may be needing a mortgage, whether it is a first mortgage or a second or third, talk to a number of lenders to get a feel for what deals are available, and what would suit your needs best. The days are long gone when your chances of getting a mortgage depended on whether and for how long you had been a saver or customer of the bank or building society. Try to see at least five, including an independent mortgage broker.

Even if you have not found the property you want to buy, it is worth talking to lenders in principle, so that you will know what mortgage you need and where to go for it when you are ready to buy a specific house.

When you have decided which lenders you want to discuss your needs with, make an appointment to see the manager or equivalent. If you just drop in, you may end up talking to someone rather inexperienced, particularly if it is on a Saturday, when things are busy.

Preparation Before you talk to potential lenders, work out what your priorities are, such as tax advantage (through a loan linked to a pension or PEP, for example), investment potential, early repayment, or cost. Try to have some idea of what you can afford by way of monthly repayments. Make a note of what life insurance cover you have got already – the information will help your lender.

Questions to ask Don't be fobbed off with a quick recommendation or offer for a homeloan without exploring all the implications and making sure you know what you would be getting. Ask if there is an arrangement fee, and how much. Find out if there is an early redemption charge. Enquire into whether a discount is offered, and ask if it makes the overall loan cheaper, or if it is a temporary benefit only. If a cashback is offered, ask about the tax implications. Check and compare the valuation report costs. If linked products like insurances are required or encouraged, perhaps as part of a package offer, check to see if they really are necessary in your circumstances, and compare prices. If insurance or investment products are involved, check what commission is payable, and to whom.

Check the small print! It is vital that you understand quite clearly what mortgage package you may be buying, why you need it for your circumstances, what will happen if things go wrong, and what it is going to cost you both in the short term and in the long term.

SOURCES OF MORTGAGES

Banks and building societies

There is little difference between the mortgages offered by banks and building societies. Their range is still rather more traditional than that of centralised lenders, which specialise in more unusual and innovative homeloans.

Along with telephone banking, some banks and building societies are moving into offering a telephone mortgage service. Because this can operate quickly and does away with the need to visit a branch, it is becoming increasingly popular, but lenders tend to require a good deposit – perhaps 20 per cent. If you are a second- or third-time buyer rather than a first-time buyer a phone mortgage may be more suitable for this reason.

Current accounts   It is common for banks to insist on mortgage borrowers opening a current account with them if they do not have one already, while building societies, the traditional lenders against properties, are unlikely to make this sort of stipulation.

Interest rate changes   Because banks borrow against the wholesale money markets, the interest rate they charge to borrowers will fluctuate (unless it is for a fixed rate loan) as and when their base lending rate changes.

Building societies, however, which rely more heavily on their savers' deposits to fund their lending, may adjust the interest rate charged for variable mortgages only once a year. This may be a benefit or a disadvantage, depending on whether rates are going up or coming down. If they are increasing, you may have several months of respite before the pain comes – but if there have been a series of rises meanwhile, the eventual change of payment can be a nasty shock. If the rate is coming down, you may have to wait longer than other borrowers to enjoy the benefit.

Centralised lenders

Centralised lenders borrow from the money markets to fund their lending, and have no need for the branch network operated by banks and building societies. They came to the fore in the mid-'80s and now account for some 7 per cent of UK mortgage business. Because of the dominant position of banks and building societies, the centralised lenders have to offer innovative products, or products for certain niche markets, like the self-employed, as well as the conventional products offered by banks and building societies.

Centralised lenders have been criticised for being slow to implement interest rate reductions but quick to introduce increases. They have also been accused of lending too easily and irresponsibly in their efforts to maximise profits, and are said to take a harsh approach to borrowers in difficulty. Some of these accusations are unfair, and centralised lenders are striving to overcome a tarnished image by offering more competitive products, rates and services, particularly for fixed rate and specialised loans.

For variable rate mortgages, banks and building societies can still be more attractive. If this is what you want, it could be worthwhile asking a centralised lender to give a guarantee that their variable interest rate will not exceed the average of the top ten building societies' rates.

Brokers and independent financial advisors

Brokers act as intermediaries between potential borrowers and mortgage providers. If they are 'tied' agents, they can only advise on the products of one bank, insurance company or building society. If they are 'independent' they should, technically, advise and recommend on every product in the marketplace. In practice, since there are hundreds of mortgage products and providers available, they will probably be knowledgeable about only a handful.

Having a broker can be useful for someone who does not have the time to shop around, or for someone who has a particular need or difficulty. You could find that your estate agent is acting on behalf of a mortgage provider, which can be useful in some circumstances.

If you decide to use a broker, it is important to ask if they will receive a fee or commission (or both) for any sale they arrange for you. You are more likely to receive unbiased and objective advice from someone who will get no commission or other benefit as result of selling you a product. There have been a number of cases of brokers selling unsuitable mortgages because they will benefit substantially from the sale.

Other mortgage providers

Until recently, the mortgage market was dominated by banks, building societies, centralised lenders and intermediaries. This has changed with the entry into homeloans provision of one of the big telephone insurers, probably with more to follow. They offer competitive products at a very competitive rate. This development is likely to mean that there will be an even greater choice available, and that it will really pay to shop around for a mortgage in future.

HOW MUCH YOU CAN BORROW

The standard calculation for working out the maximum mortgage that you will be allowed is, for one borrower, three times his or her gross annual salary; for a joint mortgage, two or two and a half times the combined salary. Some lenders will be more flexible, and it is worth asking if you want more than these limits would seem to allow. But be careful that your income can meet the increased payments.

The deposit

Not unnaturally, the bigger the deposit you can afford to put down on a property, the happier the lender will be. However, if it looks as though there is no particular credit risk, some lenders are prepared to offer 100 per cent mortgages in certain cases, both to first-time buyers and to those with existing mortgages. It will probably be necessary to demonstrate a sufficient income stream, and the survey result on the soundness of the property will be important.

A maximum mortgage of this sort can be invaluable for people with negative equity in their existing home – in other words, where the value of their home is worth less than the outstanding mortgage, as a result of a drop in property prices. Some lenders have devised various ways of coping with this sort of deficit to enable existing or new borrowers to move house (*see* Negative Equity – Your options, page 10), and so don't be deterred from thinking about a move, even if you are in a negative equity situation; it could well be worth asking around if and how lenders could help.

Information required about you

Lenders will want to know standard information about you and also your partner, if you want a joint mortgage. This will include your present address, employment details, income and outgoings, how much you want to borrow and what deposit you may put down.

They will want to know if you intend to carry out major alterations to the property other than redecoration, since this could affect the value of the property. You may also need a medical examination, depending on your state of health and past history. The lender may pay for this.

It is likely that a lender which is considering offering you a mortgage will check with one of the credit reference agencies to confirm that you have no debt problems now or in the recent past. They may also check with your employer and that of your partner to confirm your salary details.

JOINT MORTGAGES

If you want a joint mortgage, as for any other shared loan you and your partner have a shared responsibility for ensuring that the necessary repayments are made. If something happens to one partner, preventing them from fulfilling their share of the repayment, then the other partner will be expected to contribute the shortfall. Otherwise, there is a danger that the property will be repossessed. Talk to your lender if there are problems.

It can happen that there is a need to offer your home as security for another financial commitment incurred by one person in a partnership. If this happens, banks and building societies are required by law to advise the other partner where there is a joint mortgage. If you find yourself in this situation, you would be strongly advised to seek independent legal advice before agreeing to it. If things go wrong with the deal, you could lose your home.

MAIN TYPES OF MORTGAGE

Endowment

With this sort of mortgage, you have to take out an endowment insurance policy which matures at the end of the mortgage and which is then used to pay off the mortgage loan in a lump sum. You have to make monthly repayments for the endowment as you would on any investment-type insurance policy. This is over and above your regular mortgage repayments, which only cover the interest due on the mortgage loan, not the capital sum borrowed for the property. There are two types of endowment mortgage:

Low-cost with profits This is the usual sort of endowment, guaranteeing to pay back part of the loan only. However, because bonuses are likely to be added, it is usually enough to pay off the loan in full.

Unit-linked endowment With this, the monthly premiums are used to buy units in investment funds. The drawback is that there is no guarantee how much the policy will be worth on maturity, since this depends on how well the investments have performed.

An endowment mortgage may be suitable for some people, but you should check carefully that it really is right for you if you are contemplating this sort of mortgage. Since it is investment-linked there is the danger that in the event of poor performance there will not be enough to pay off the mortgage when the time comes.

Also, because they are expensive products generating a sizeable commission for the broker or salesman involved in arranging the endowment mortgage, there could be a temptation for the broker to recommend an endowment instead of a less lucrative but more suitable alternative. Before you make your decision, ask them what they will make from the deal for themselves. Under new commission disclosure rules they are required by law to tell you.

Finally, if you change your mortgage and decide you do not wish to continue with an endowment mortgage, and so cash in the endowment policy early, you will almost certainly get a poor return unless it is close to maturity. In the early years of the policy, most of your contributions will go towards administration charges and commission, rather than making money for you straight away. The alternative in these circumstances is to maintain the endowment until it matures, treating it as a stand-alone investment product which hopefully will make some money for you in due course.

Repayment mortgages This is another popular sort of mortgage, under which the borrower makes monthly repayments, paying back the loan and the interest over the duration of the mortgage. It is the least risky because it is not linked to investment performance, only to the current mortgage rate. Repayment mortgages allow a degree of flexibility. For example, you may wish to extend the term of the mortgage, or to pay the interest only, if you have difficulty making repayments for a while. Another advantage is that, as long as the required repayments are made, the mortgage is guaranteed to be paid off at the end of its term.

However, if you are someone who moves house every five years or so, then a repayment mortgage may not be the best one for you. With a repayment mortgage, you pay interest every month but only a small proportion of the capital, particularly in the early years of the mortgage. So, after a few years you will have paid off only a fraction of the loan; if you move regularly, increasing the loan as you do, then you may find you have paid off very little of the total capital sum at the end of it all. An endowment mortgage or one based on investments, while more risky, could be better for you under these circumstances since you can transfer the plan from property to property, while it can, hopefully, grow steadily as it matures.

Most lenders calculate the reducing capital balance annually, while a few lenders calculate this on a monthly basis – which can result in quite a saving for the borrower over the period of the mortgage. It could be worthwhile checking with lenders as to their policy on this when you are looking for your mortgage.

PEP mortgages

With this sort of mortgage, the borrower pays interest on the homeloan, but also makes contributions to a PEP (Personal Equity Plan), which should pay off the mortgage. Because the PEP is investment-linked, there is no guarantee that there will be enough profit to do this.

In general, however, a PEP mortgage is a flexible and tax-efficient way of saving to repay the capital on a mortgage, since PEPs are free of income tax and capital gains tax. They are becoming increasingly popular as a mortgage vehicle, and are more widely available from lenders. If you have trouble finding a lender for a PEP mortgage, some unit trust groups have made arrangements with lenders so that funds are available if you choose one of their PEPs.

Pension mortgage

While the borrower pays interest on the loan, he or she also contributes to a personal pension plan, which is tax-free. When you take your pension, some of it goes as a tax-free lump sum to repay the mortgage.

Again, pension mortgages depend on investment performance, and if this has not been good then there may not be enough to pay off the mortgage. Also, unlike an endowment or a PEP, you cannot cash in a pension plan early. The advantages are that you get tax relief on pension contributions at your highest rate, and the cash fund is tax-free.

Interest-only mortgage

The borrower pays interest only on the loan, and decides for himself how he or she will repay the loan itself, and when. The lender will want to know how ultimately you plan to repay the capital sum which remains outstanding.

Mixed mortgage

A new development is that one or two lenders now allow borrowers to mix a combination of mortgages in one deal, customising the mortgage to suit each individual.

Foreign currency mortgage

Some foreign banks offer short-term mortgages in the foreign currency of that bank. Their lending criteria can be much more relaxed than trying to borrow from a British lender. However, the advantage of this sort of mortgage depends on currency fluctuations: if the pound is stable or rises, the borrower benefits. If the pound drops, the borrower will have to pay more.

These are probably the most risky homeloans there are since you are gambling on currency movements. They are for sophisticated investors only, who understand the fluctuations and volatility of the money markets and who have reserves to call on if it becomes necessary.

MORTGAGE PAYMENT PLANS

Fixed-term mortgages

Fixed-term mortgages have their interest rate set for a certain period of time, usually between one and five years, or ten at the most, after which the rate will revert to a variable rate, like other mortgages. Generally speaking, the shorter the duration of the fixed-rate mortgage, the lower the interest rate and vice versa. They are becoming increasingly popular as borrowers have seen or experienced, perhaps to their cost, the massive changes in interest rates – up and down – over the last few years.

Fixed-term mortgages can be very good value, and they certainly bring peace of mind in that you know exactly what you will pay each month for a set period of time, without worrying about fluctuations in bank base rates affecting your mortgage rate. They are good for people who like to budget as precisely and long term as possible. The disadvantage is that they are a gamble. If interest rates rise, then you will benefit, but if they come down then you will lose.

While fixed mortgages can be transferred from one property to another, you can only do this if the lender approves the survey of your new home. Also, there may be penalties and your fixed-rate mortgage may be withdrawn if the sale of your old home and the purchase of the new one are not within a month of each other.

If, as a result of moving house, you change your mortgage altogether during the term of a fixed-rate mortgage, then there may be heavy penalties, usually as much as one month's interest for every year of the fixed period.

Variable mortgages

A variable mortgage is one where the interest rate charged by the lender may move to correspond with changes in bank base rates. If the change is very small, then it may not be adjusted at all. If the change is significant, then the mortgage rate will certainly move. Building societies will reflect any interest changes once a year, while other lenders will impose the adjustment as or soon after the base rate moves.

Rates charged by lenders vary considerably, and can be affected by add-on costs (*see* Tie-Ins and Other Costs, pages 70-2). Apparent discounts and cashbacks can disguise higher interest rates, or be short term only. Some lenders also charge penalties for redeeming a mortgage mid-month. It is important to read the small print.

Discounted mortgages

Because of the competitive nature of the mortgage market, some lenders may offer a discount to first-time buyers in particular if they buy a mortgage package. If you already have a mortgage with a lender, they may offer you a discount if you change your mortgage because of a move, and stay with them.

Discounts are normally 1–2 per cent off the lender's standard mortgage rate for one year. There are disadvantages in having a discount: one is that you may be required to take out insurance, and another is that the interest rate when the discount period ends may be higher than you would have got elsewhere, eliminating any saving achieved by the discount.

Capped mortgages

Some lenders offer schemes whereby the interest rate is capped; in other words, there is a guarantee that it will not rise above a certain level, whatever the base rate is. Again, this sort of scheme is normally for a limited period of time only.

Cashback schemes

Some lenders have been offering 'cashback' schemes to potential borrowers in order to get their custom in an increasingly competitive marketplace. These are cash incentives to new borrowers, ranging from a few hundred pounds to perhaps £6,000 from certain building societies. These schemes indicate, perhaps, the margins available to lenders who can afford to give away large sums to attract new borrowers on to the variable rate.

Cashback deals may not be as good as they seem, in that borrowers could by shopping around get a better deal elsewhere through a fixed rate or even a discount. Additionally, where there are sizeable cashbacks involved, there could be an eventual tax liability implication, according to recent hints from the Inland Revenue. If you are attracted by a cashback scheme, check carefully what hidden penalties, if any, could arise.

On the plus side, cashback offers, and discounts, can be so attractive from certain lenders that it is worthwhile thinking about getting a re-mortgage to get the one or the other. If you are on a fixed-rate mortgage, then the penalties for early redemption would mean that savings would be unlikely. For variable-rate mortgages, however, it could be worthwhile checking with your lender to see if a change could bring about significant savings.

Mixed schemes

Just as borrowers can choose a combination of pension, endowment or repayment if they wish, so one or two lenders will allow a choice between fixed-, variable- or capped-rate mortgages, to suit their circumstances. While this opportunity may appeal to people who like the idea of an investment element in their loan, it may not be suitable for a borrower whose mortgage is linked to an endowment policy coming to maturity.

Some lenders also allow a choice of when to pay, and how much. Borrowers may choose to pay the loan fortnightly, for example, which is the equivalent of making one extra repayment a year, or to inject a lump sum of any size at any time to reduce the loan.

Paying extra

For most people, their mortgage is their biggest financial commitment, and the idea of reducing it or paying it off altogether is very attractive. When inflation is low, and mortgage tax relief is shrinking, it pays to reduce your mortgage as quickly as possible.

Lenders used to be very rigid in their acceptance of unusual repayment patterns, but the increasing competition to provide homeloans, and homeloans that are tailored to individuals' personal circumstances, has required them to come up with and to accept innovative ways of paying for a homeloan.

Extra contributions The idea of injecting occasional or extra contributions into homeloans is growing in acceptability among lenders, and a number are prepared, for example, to accept payments every two weeks instead of once a month. This will mean thirteen payments instead of twelve over the year, so the mortgage will be paid off earlier than expected.

Maintaining payment levels Another option is that, when interest rates come down, instead of accepting the automatic reduction effected in your payments by the lender, you ask the lender to maintain the original level of repayment. Not only does this reduce the mortgage more quickly but it also means that, if rates go up, you have a buffer to cushion the effects of the rise.

Building societies It is important, if you wish to enhance your mortgage payments either through regular payments or through occasional lump sums, to get the arrangement set up properly. If you are borrowing from a lender who changes the terms annually only, such as a building society, you can arrange to put extra cash into a building society account during the year to accrue interest and for it to be credited to your mortgage account at the end of the year. There would be unlikely to be any charge for this. This is useful if you wish to make small additional payments.

Banks Other lenders, such as banks, who are able to adjust terms and conditions more rapidly, are normally pleased to accept occasional or regular lump sums, and to credit them against the mortgage at that time. It is important, however, to make it clear to such lenders that the lump sum is not a pre-payment but must be treated as an injection against the mortgage immediately. If you do decide to increase your mortgage payments, inform your lender in advance and in writing why and when you are sending extra money.

Minimum capital repayment Bear in mind that some lenders impose a minimum capital repayment, perhaps £500–£1,000 a year, and will not accept smaller amounts.

Fixed-rate mortgages If you have a fixed-rate mortgage, early capital repayments can incur penalties, and so you should not make any overpayments until the end of the fixed period. You should also bear in mind that it may not be so easy if you have an endowment mortgage to make an early repayment, since the payment term is fixed at the beginning and cannot normally be shortened.

Intermediaries One or two companies have introduced schemes whereby, for a sum of about £200, they will arrange for homeowners to cancel their monthly mortgage payments and re-route them through a new bank account, to enable the borrowers to make half their monthly payments during the course of a year. Thus 13 payments would be made instead of the normal 12, reducing the mortgage commensurately.

In fact, there is no need to use a middleman to achieve this result. Most lenders would be happy to set up such a scheme free of charge. While it is very sensible to pay extra to reduce the mortgage, by using an intermediary you are spending money unnecessarily to provide commission and perks to financial advisers recommending the scheme.

TIE-INS

Lenders may insist, or encourage strongly, that you buy products, usually to do with insurance of some sort, as a condition of letting you have a homeloan, particularly where a discount is involved. While it can be convenient to be able to purchase all your housing needs in one package, there can be drawbacks. They can be more expensive, for example, and you may not necessarily need all the add-ons included. These are the main 'tie-in' products.

Building and contents insurance

These are the most common ties, and many lenders insist that you buy buildings insurance, in particular, through them. This can prove more expensive than choosing your own insurance package and it is worthwhile comparing prices with other providers. Indeed, some insurance agreements insist that homeowners insure their house contents for a large minimum sum – say, £40,000 – which may be more than some people's homes are worth.

However, be warned – some lenders may charge you if you try to buy buildings and contents insurance from another company. Sometimes this charge will wipe out altogether the benefit of any saving through going elsewhere.

Mortgage protection insurance or term insurance This normally applies to repayment or pension mortgages only. Lenders may insist on a borrower taking out this sort of mortgage protection, which repays the loan if you die within the term of the mortgage. It is a good recommendation to consider taking out this sort of policy if you have dependants.

Redundancy insurance Redundancy insurance may be compulsory from some lenders for certain packages. It can be comforting to have this in times of employment uncertainty; but check it out carefully before you take it. It can be expensive, and may offer only limited help with repayments for a fairly short period of time.

Mortgage indemnity policy This can also be compulsory, which seems a bit unfair since it protects the lender and not you, insuring them against loss if they have to repossess your home and then sell it for less than the mortgage outstanding. It can be expensive and may involve a one-off fee of several hundred pounds on a £50,000 loan for a home worth £55,000, for example. It is normally charged on properties where you are borrowing over 80 per cent of their value, depending on the lender.

Payment protection insurance This insurance will cover your repayments if you become ill, unemployed or have an accident.

Personal pension or endowment policies These may be part of a discounted mortgage package. While the package may seem superficially attractive, remember that the discount is usually short term while the endowment or pension commitment is long term, and so any saving you make at first may be eliminated by the overall costs. Unless you are set on one of these mortgages, compare the long-term costs of a repayment or other different mortgage scheme before making your decision.

OTHER COSTS

Because of the growing number of add-ons involved in buying a mortgage, it is not always easy to compare the options available to get the best deal and most suitable mortgage product for you. The Annual Percentage Rate (APR) was intended to allow borrowers to compare different offers of credit, including mortgages, so that they could work out reasonably easily what was the best deal for them.

However, because some costs do not need to be included in the APR calculation, such as tax relief, mortgage indemnity premiums, tied-in insurance, or premiums for endowment policies, pension plans and mortgage protection, or can be disguised, the APR figure should be treated as an indicator only, and you should check all the expenses involved in getting a mortgage with prospective lenders.

These are some of the other hidden extras you should look for, over and above the tie-ins discussed above:

- **Arrangement fees** are increasingly often being charged by lenders on fixed-rate mortgages, and this fee is not always clearly disclosed. Ask about it at the outset.
- **Valuation report fees** Lenders insist upon a valuation before offering a homeloan, and it is unusual for them to allow the customer to choose his or her own surveyor. The cost of the valuation report arranged by the bank may be more than if they had commissioned their own valuation report from the same firm, or another one of their choice.
- **Reference fees** may be charged by lenders when a borrower needs a reference from another bank or building society. They may range from £10 to £50 or more. Furthermore, some public sector employers, such as local authorities and health trusts, impose a charge for providing a mortgage reference on their employees, which the lender will usually pass on to the borrower.
- **Redemption penalties** are likely to be charged if you swap to another lender during the term of a fixed-rate or discounted mortgage, and they can be heavy.

PAYING OFF YOUR MORTGAGE

Tax relief

For a long time mortgage tax relief was a really good benefit, particularly for higher-rate taxpayers. More recently, however, the rates have diminished considerably, to 15 per cent in 1995, and it looks as if it is a perk that is withering on the vine. Despite this, old perceptions linger, and people still tend to think that it is a good idea to keep a mortgage of £30,000 going just for the tax benefit it provides.

This is no longer true. It could be worthwhile to pay off the mortgage altogether in certain circumstances, particularly at a time of low inflation, and to invest the money that would otherwise have been used for repayments into a high-interest savings account. Speak to your bank or building society, or financial advisor, if this could apply to you.

There are, as always, exceptions to this rule. Mortgage finance, because it is securitised on your home, is one of the cheapest forms of finance there is. So, while it is good to pay off your mortgage, you may be advised to retain it in whole or in part if by repaying it you find yourself with the need to borrow at a higher rate for some large expense. You could consider, perhaps, reducing it by a half or a third, which would still leave you with a reserve and also cut down your outgoings.

If you decide to pay off your mortgage in whole or in part, check with your lender in case there are any penalties for early repayment as a result of taking a fixed-rate loan, a cashback or a social discount. You should also check to see when is the best time to make the repayment, to ensure your money does not sit with the lender earning no interest for you.

Cash or mortgage?

If you come into money, through either a policy maturing or inheritance, perhaps, you may wish to consider whether you should pay off the mortgage or, instead, invest the lump sum. In these circumstances, you should estimate what your current mortgage is costing you, and if you could get a better return elsewhere, taking into account the risk factors involved in investing in different investment vehicles.

You may also wish to consider if you want the peace of mind of paying off what has probably been a significant debt, or to have the freedom and flexibility of having cash available. Unless you are an experienced professional or investor, I would suggest that you take expert advice in these circumstances.

Closure charges

It can come as quite a shock for people who pay off their mortgage completely to discover that some lenders will charge an administration fee. This should not be confused with early redemption penalties, which have been discussed earlier.

The charge is likely to cover any costs involved in closing down the mortgage account, and also for sending the borrower his deeds, and a 'sealing charge'. Check with your lender what their policy is, and see if they will hold the deeds for you free of charge after closure.

Otherwise, you may want to think about leaving a very small amount outstanding in your mortgage account – even £1 – so that you can borrow more should you need to, but will miss out on the administration fee. You would not have to pay interest. Check, though, that your lender is not one of the few that require you to keep a larger minimum sum in your account. Some stipulate that you must have at least £500 in your account.

COMPLAINING IF SOMETHING GOES WRONG

Legal rights

The sort of redress you get will depend on what type of mortgage you have, and how you obtained it. If you have a plan that involves investment or life insurance, such as an endowment, PEP or pension mortgage, then that element of the plan is covered by the Financial Services Act. The FSA, as it is known, regulates the sale of investment products very strictly, and the procedures are outlined later in this section.

Mortgage advice and lending are not protected by the FSA, except where investments are involved. So, repayment mortgages are not covered at all in this context. There are ways to seek redress, and these are described later, but the equivalent legal recourse does not exist at the moment.

Taking action

Because mortgages are getting increasingly complicated, it is important to know exactly what you are buying, and to be confident that your mortgage plan is the right one for your circumstances. The beginning of this chapter explained what you should think about when looking for a homeloan.

If you suspect after you have taken out the loan that it was not appropriate, and you feel you were wrongly advised, it is important to take action straightaway, because it can take a long time to sort it out and get redress, if this is justified. Ensure that you have as much specific evidence as possible, because the more evidence you can produce, the greater are your chances of compensation.

The rules on giving financial advice have been tightened up recently, to ensure that customers are given as much information about what they are buying as possible, in a form that is easily understood. It is up to you to make sure that you know what you are buying. Lenders won't mind if you ask numerous questions about their mortgage products, and it is in your interest to do so.

Don't be pressurised by the speed of the buying and selling process to make a hasty decision that could be costly and that you could regret later. If there is a dispute at a later stage about the suitability of what you bought, and the lender is able to prove that you were given the minimum information necessary but did not check the small print, or that you omitted some relevant personal information at the time, then you could be found to be at fault if something goes wrong.

Problems with insurance/investment advice

Probably the most common complaint about insurance and investment advice in connection with mortgages is to do with endowments. Endowments are a major source of profit to the product provider and the broker, and there have been cases where endowment mortgages were recommended where these were in fact unsuitable, or borrowers were recommended to surrender an endowment policy and take out a new one with a new mortgage, which would benefit the lender or broker only.

If you believe that you were given bad advice about anything to do with the insurance or investment part of a mortgage, particularly where you lost money or paid too much, then you should approach the following organisations, in this order, in writing, for help. Do not write to them simultaneously, as this would only muddle the process!

- **The company** that sold you the product
- **Personal Investment Authority (PIA,** which is an organisation responsible for regulating lenders and individuals who give advice on and sell insurance and investment products)
- **The PIA Ombudsman,** who can investigate any firm registered with PIA

You could also write to:

- **Securities and Investment Board** (which supervises PIA)
- **Insurance Ombudsman** (which is a Government-appointed consumer watchdog which investigates complaints from individuals, and decides who is right or wrong)
- **Investment Ombudsman** if your problem is to do with investment products

Problems with mortgage advice

If you believe you were sold the wrong sort of mortgage, then you should approach your lender and ask them to switch it to the more appropriate one without charge. Write to your branch first, if this was done through a bank or building society, and then to the Head Office if you are not happy with their response.

If this does not work either, then you could write to the Building Societies' Ombudsman or the Banking Ombudsman as appropriate.

For general guidance and advice about mortgages, the Building Society Association or the British Bankers' Association have free publications that should help you. Additionally, the Consumers' Association Publication, *Which?* runs regular articles about what to look for in a mortgage.

CHAPTER 5

Buying and Selling in Scotland

Scotland has its own system of law, so buying and selling a house or flat is quite a different process from doing so in England, Wales or Northern Ireland.

BUYING A HOUSE OR FLAT

The system works more quickly and although there is far less risk of gazumping, an active market can be more competitive.

Looking for property

Solicitors' property centres and offices These are the largest source of properties available in Scotland. Often found in town centres, the property centres provide property information in a similar way to estate agents outside Scotland. Although the staff are not solicitors themselves, they can help with basic details. If you are interested in a property you get in touch with the solicitor selling it.

Like estate agents, the centres often publish newsletters containing details of current properties. It's a good idea to be put on mailing lists for these, particularly if you are buying from a distance. The Law Society of Scotland can give you details of solicitors' property centres.

Newspapers Daily Scottish newspapers are a good source of property. The papers are usually regional so find out what day the property section is published for the paper in the area of interest. Local newspapers are also useful.

Estate agents   Estate agents in Scotland are often part of recognised chains and offer very much the same services as those in England.

First steps to buying

It's a good idea to organise your mortgage with a lender and to contact a solicitor for legal advice before looking at houses. Things can move quite quickly once you find a suitable property. Surveys are undertaken before any formal offer is made, so you'll have to be prepared and ready to enlist the services of the appropriate professionals.

Ownership of property

Property in Scotland does not exist as freehold or leasehold as it does elsewhere. Instead, a system called 'feudal tenure' exists. This means that, as in freehold, the owner has rights to the building and the land. However, the original owner of the development still has some say over any alterations and use of the land. There may be restrictions on the use of the property; and for any alterations or extensions, consent is always required.

These feuing conditions are permanent and should be checked before purchase is considered. The details of any conditions will appear on the title document held by the current owner or his mortgage lender.

A new owner (feuar) can negotiate to have conditions waived, but there may be a charge for this. It may cost you more than you anticipate for simply erecting a garage. Further details of the system can be obtained from the Lands Tribunal for Scotland or your solicitor.

The feudal tenure also applies to flats, so that all shared areas, including the roof, the ground upon which they are built, and common services, are owned equally by the residents. The costs of

---

At the Same Time

As well as differences in house-buying procedures, Scottish law has different principles for inheritance. While you are having dealings with a solicitor it is a good idea to clarify wills and inheritance.

repairs and maintenance are shared. Details of apportionment are covered in the title deeds.

House prices

Property in Scotland is normally sold as 'offers over' (sometimes called the 'upset price'); the price set is usually the minimum and may not be negotiated down. This method is used where the property is likely to prove popular and to get the best price.

If a quick sale is required a property may be sold as 'fixed price'; the seller will take the first offer at that price.

If there is more than one prospective purchaser the seller may opt to set a 'closing date' for offers. The process is then like a blind bid, with none of the buyers knowing the price anyone else is offering. Although the seller usually accepts the highest price, this is not always the case; other factors, such as the date of entry, may be taken into consideration.

The Buying process

This flow chart shows the main stages of buying a house or flat.

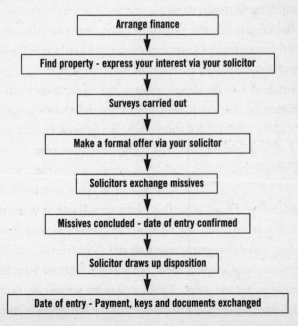

Surveys These are carried out before a formal offer is made. In some instances it means that you may pay for a survey on a house you can't purchase because your offer is not accepted.

There are no licensed conveyancers in Scotland. All the legal work is dealt with by solicitors. Because solicitors are so

Costs of moving in Scotland
- Legal fees payable to your solicitor
- Stamp Duty
- Mortgage
  Indemnity insurance (see p. 15)
  Arrangement fees (see p. 15)
- Registration of ownership at the Registrar

involved in the buying process you will probably find they will arrange surveys so discuss exactly what you want at the start.

The types of survey available are similar to those in England and Wales. **A valuation report** means just that; its main purpose is to provide the money lender with details of the true market value. The surveyor will look at the structure of the property and, if there are any major doubts, may suggest further detailed surveys. The report is for the lender and, unless you have arranged to include the valuation with a structural survey, will not necessarily be disclosed to you.

Home Buyer's Survey and Valuation is the same procedure as suggested by the Royal Institution of Chartered Surveyors (*see* pages 53-4). It is the minimum structural survey that should be considered.

Full structural (or building) surveys are less common in Scotland, mainly because of the speed at which house purchases progress. Sellers often don't allow a full survey unless there is a limited market or the buyer expresses a strong interest. But it is highly recommended for very old or individual properties.

Making an offer Your interest in buying a house is relayed via your solicitor to the selling solicitor by word of mouth. It does not have any legal standing and either party may pull out.

If the surveys are satisfactory then your solicitor will take your instructions about making a formal offer. Dealing should always be through your solicitor, although you may discuss things such as fittings to be included with the seller. The letter offering to buy forms part of the sale contract and should include all the conditions of the purchase, fixtures and fittings and a proposed 'date of entry' which is the date you would like to move into the house.

Exchange of missives   If the offer is accepted, a formal letter called qualified acceptance is returned by the seller's solicitor, confirming or amending the conditions. The entry date may need to be negotiated to suit both parties (see below). These formal letters are referred to as 'missives' and may go back and forth for clarification. It can take over two weeks sometimes for the conditions to be agreed, or as little as a few days if there are no complications.

Missives concluded   Once all the conditions are agreed, the purchase is then legally binding for both buyer and seller. The missives are concluded by the acting solicitors; neither the buyer nor the seller signs anything.

There is no deposit paid in the Scottish system except if you are buying a new house from a property developer.

The law states that once the missives have been concluded, the purchaser is responsible for the insurance of the property. However, it is more usual for an agreement to be made in the missives that the seller remains liable until the date of entry.

Date of entry   The date that you would like to move is suggested in your formal offer to the seller. It may obviously have to be negotiated to fit in with all concerned but is normally set between one and two months after the offer is made. In this time you should be able to sell your house and complete any legal work.

Disposition   Before the date of entry, your solicitor will prepare a disposition to confirm the change of ownership. He will obtain from the seller's solicitor the title deeds which will be signed by the seller to agree the change of ownership. These will be handed over on the date of entry, following payment of the property price.

Searches There are two types of searches in Scotland:

- Immediately prior to exchanging missives a search on the property and against the individual is made. This checks that the seller has a good title to the property and that the purchaser can grant security for the loan.
- A local authority search forms part of the missives. It checks that there are no proposed developments that would affect the property.

SELLING A HOUSE OR FLAT

If you already own a house in Scotland, your experience from buying it should have given you some idea of Scottish law relating to the housing market. You may also be in the process of purchasing another property in Scotland and will therefore be involved on both sides.

Ways of selling your house

The majority of houses are bought and sold through solicitors' offices, but you also have the options of selling through an estate agent or selling it privately yourself. Whichever option you choose, it is customary in Scotland to show prospective buyers around the house and explain the details.

DIY selling This involves setting the price, preparing the sales details about the house, advertising it and showing people around. You will have to pay for any advertising, for example in local papers. The advantage of a DIY sale is that you save on the commission charged by a solicitor or estate agent. However, use a solicitor to check that the particulars are accurate.

Setting the price Look around at the prices similar properties are selling for or have a surveyor carry out a valuation for you, which will cost about £70. Choose a surveyor who is regularly involved in house valuation so that the valuation is accurate.

Remember Set a realistic purchase price, as a potential purchaser will check

BUYING AND SELLING IN SCOTLAND 83

the market value to secure a loan. Setting a price too low may invite interest which is then lost when a true valuation and surveys are carried out.

Using a solicitor You will need the services of a solicitor to deal with any offers and to exchange missives. You should never personally get into discussions about offers – pass the buyer on to your solicitor.

For further details on DIY selling *see* Chapter 7, Selling Your Home

Selling through an estate agent These are normally Scottish branches of well-known chains of estate agents. They offer a service similar to their English counterparts.

In contrast to selling through a solicitor, estate agents often encourage you to take the first offer rather than generating interest and setting a closing date.

Any offers made on your house will be handed on to your solicitor by the selling agent.

As with most processes in buying or selling a house it is a good idea to get several quotes before contracting a professional, and to check exactly what they are offering you.

Costs are normally around $1^{1}/_{2}$ per cent of the final selling price. Some may also charge for extra advertising such as appearing in an estate agent's newspaper.

Selling through a solicitor Most property in Scotland is sold through solicitors. They provide a service similar to estate agents and have property centres displaying details of houses for sale, although there may be an extra one-off charge for this depending on the area you are in. Their commission charges are often slightly cheaper than those of estate agents. It is normal practice to use the same solicitor to sell your house and carry out the legal involvement with the sale.

The selling process
Your solicitor or estate agent will prepare the sales particulars and discuss the selling price with you as part of their contract. Depending upon the

circumstances, they will advise as to whether the house is sold as 'offers above' or as 'fixed price'.

The 'offers above' or 'upset price' is usually set slightly below the expected price to encourage buyers. If a degree of competitiveness is created you may be able to set a 'closing date', (*see* Accepting Offers, below) which usually achieves a better selling price.

In drawing up sales particulars, either yourself or with a solicitor or estate agent, make it clear what items are to be included with the sale and whether they are taken into account in the advertised price.

Fixtures and fittings, such as carpets, curtains or kitchen equipment, will be attractive to some purchasers. Make sure they have a full list of what is included in the price. Legally you should leave all fixtures and fittings, unless you draw up a contract stating otherwise. Fixtures and fittings are defined as anything that would require a screwdriver to remove, but if you are not clear on what you can take or should leave, consult your solicitor before setting a price.

The legal services of your solicitor   There are two main areas the solicitor will need to follow up to allow smooth progress with a house sale. It cannot be stressed enough that a Scottish sale requires the services of a solicitor from the start, unlike the English system.

- The title deeds will be examined to check that you are the true owner of the property. Scottish law includes the Matrimonial Homes (Family Protection) (Scotland) Act; even if only one spouse owns the property, permission to sell must be given by the partner.
- Conveyancing will involve property surveys, and local searches to check there are no proposals for developments.

If you are using the solicitor to sell your house, they may offer an overall charge that covers selling and legal services.

Accepting offers

Your solicitor will tell you if anyone has shown an interest in your property. The buyer will then need to have a survey carried out before a formal offer is made.

If a lot of interest is shown in your house, you could consider setting a 'closing date' for offers. Your solicitor or estate agent should advise whether this is a good idea. There is no point in setting a date until you are sure more than one person is likely to make a formal offer.

The closing date is a specific time on a particular day that all formal offers will be assessed. You are not obliged to accept any of the offers if they are too low. Nor does the highest offer have to be accepted. If the offers are similar you may find one of them more favourable in terms of suggested entry dates or other factors. You don't have to accept any but could re-advertise instead.

If you accept the highest offer, your solicitor may negotiate points concerning other conditions, such as extras included or dates, but there must be no attempt to try to raise the price offered.

If you are using an estate agent, their role ends once the offer has been handed over to the solicitor.

A formal offer will include all the conditions of the sale, the price, any items included, and the date of entry. Some offers are made with a time limit in which you must accept verbally, which can be as little as within 24 hours. You should seek advice from your solicitor whether to act promptly. You may be advised to hold out for a higher offer. If a purchaser is seriously interested they will not mind waiting for an acceptance.

Your solicitor will engage in the process of exchanging missives with the buyer's solicitor. Missives are formal letters laying down conditions of sale and may be passed back and forth until an amicable agreement is reached. Once final missives have been exchanged the contract is legally binding for both parties, so it is important that you are familiar with all the conditions being negotiated by your solicitor through the missives. It will be too late once they have finally been exchanged.

Setting an entry date The date for finalising the sale is suggested by both the seller and by the buyer in his offer. It is negotiated by both parties, and a mutually agreed date is written into the missives. This is the date when the keys are handed to your solicitor, and you must move out. Although the date of entry is set by the seller it may need to be changed to achieve a compromise which suits you and the purchaser. An entry date set too far ahead can cost you in bridging loans, but may be all right if a higher offer compensates for this.

Completion of the sale Following the exchange of missives, your solicitor will tie up the final details for the date of entry.

Title deeds Your buyer's solicitor will need to prepare the 'disposition' and for this your solicitor will send the title deeds. The disposition is the document that states the change of ownership on the title deeds, and will need to be signed by you. It is handed over to the purchaser's solicitor in exchange for payment of the property on the date of settlement.

Confirming finance Your lender will be told that missives have be encompleted and will be informed with an indication of the price so that your lender knows how much of the existing loan will be repaid.

Discharge document The solicitor prepares a discharge document that will be signed by the seller's lender before the date of entry.

Handing over keys This will be arranged between you and your solicitor, but it is usual for you to hand the keys to your solicitor on the date of entry. Never hand over keys directly to the purchaser, particularly if you have already vacated the property. It is usual that you have to maintain the insurance and condition of the house until the date of entry. The purchaser can take action if the house is not in the condition agreed in the sale contract so you don't want anyone entering without your supervision. It has also been known for purchasers to delay payment once they have the keys. The solicitor should hand keys over on redemption of payment, unless he is supervising a visit to measure up for the purchaser's fittings.

Payment Your solicitor will be in possession of the cheque from the purchaser on the settlement date. From this he will deduct his fees, pay off the loan from your lender and any bridging loan, and give you a cheque for any remaining balance. Make sure you receive a statement at the same time detailing all the financial exchanges. Remember that it will take time for cheques to clear through the banking system and this should be taken into account if you are depending upon the money for another purchase.

CHAPTER 6

Having a Self-build House

Having a house built for you or by you, where you want and the way you want it, is not difficult or expensive. It is fast becoming a popular way of finding the right home, and you don't actually need to touch a shovel or brick.

One in every three detached houses built today, in the UK, is a self-build project. The most popular size is a four-bedroom rural or semi-rural house, but self-build is not just for those looking for a 'mansion'; there are plenty of companies with sample plans and styles ranging from large family homes to simple single-storey houses.

There are many advantages to self-build:

- You can plan the rooms yourself and decide the exact size and type of house you want.
- From a cost point of view, self-build could save you around a third of the finished value of the property, if not more, depending upon who builds the house for you. There are a lot of companies who will arrange the building for you or you could employ your own contractors; the latter usually works out the cheapest way.
- You have the opportunity of owning a larger house than you could afford if you were buying an existing property.
- Modern conveniences such as built-in vacuum cleaning systems, energy-efficient heating systems such as underfloor heating and optimum insulation can be incorporated to keep running costs down.

- You could have a basement built at the same time to give extra space.

The most common hurdles, and sometimes expenses, are finding suitable land with planning permission, and the time involved.

From obtaining planning permission, a self-build project can take between six and twelve months, but it depends very much on how you organise the project.

Self-builders are usually entering a field of which they have no practical knowledge. It is important to seek good professional advice from the start and to research all the possible options fully.

With all this in mind, you will need to consider a range of options and make a lot of decisions. Plans, materials such as flooring, roofing, and fittings such as windows, doors and kitchen units need to be thought out. Aspects which are normally standard when buying an existing property have to be considered, even down to the garden plan and driveway. Self-build is not for the indecisive!

GETTING STARTED

Costs

You will need to consider the financial implications right from the start. A rough breakdown of the costs involved includes:

- Purchasing land with planning permission. On average self-builders spend from £25,000 to £50,000 on the land. If all this sounds way beyond your means, don't be put off, as the costs vary considerably depending upon where you are looking to build. Many self-builders are able to use land they already have, such as within an existing large garden.
- Professional fees: using an architect to draw plans, a conveyancer and other costs associated with buying a house such as arranging a mortgage.
- Labour costs will vary, depending upon whether you use a sole contractor or employ your own subcontractors. If you can do some of the work yourself it will keep the building costs down.

- The cost of materials will vary depending upon your specifications; higher levels of insulation or quality of materials will be more expensive.
- Additional costs including service connections, insurance, landscaping, and possibly special foundations or creating new access.

You should also consider how you are going to finance the build and find somewhere to live in the meantime. You may have to sell your current house to afford the mortgage on the house you are building.

Help at hand

There are specialist magazines (e.g., *Build It* and *Individual Homes*) for self-build enthusiasts. These are a good source of ideas, showing you what other people have achieved and what's on offer. The houses range from extravagant country homes down to budget-builds. Another good source for help and ideas are *Building Your Own Home*, *Plans for Dream Homes* and *Home Plans* available by mail order from Ryton Books or from any good bookshop (*see* Useful Addresses).

Exhibitions are an ideal way to discuss ideas and meet suppliers. Annual shows include the *Build It* show at Alexandra Palace, London, in the second week of September, and the *Individual Homes* Exhibition in the spring. There are also local regional shows. Details can be found in the specialist magazines.

For independent advice, experts in their fields can be contacted through the National Self-Build Helpline (*see* Useful Addresses).

For self-builders who are actually taking on a lot of the practical element themselves, the Association of Self Builders (annual membership £18) is made up of members with hands-on experience. Ideas can be exchanged at local meetings or through the newsletter. The Association is non-profit-making, but offers benefits to its members, such as special discounts for materials and services including discounted insurance.

Constructive Individuals, a small company set up to help self-builders, offers training seminars in project management and basic practical skills for those who want to get their hands dirty.

The Individual House Builders' Association is made up of member companies associated with the industry. They promote the industry and can provide a handbook (£35) for self-builders which covers aspects ranging from design to choosing doors and windows.

Elements involved in self-build

Most self-build projects comprise the following stages, but not necessarily in this order:

Some self-build package companies may take responsibility for all the areas given below, if you wish.

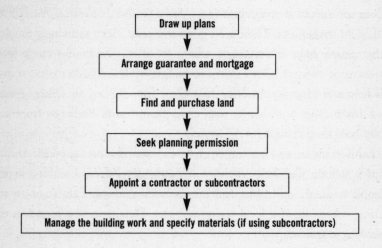

```
            ┌──────────────────────────┐
            │      Draw up plans       │
            └──────────────────────────┘
                        │
        ┌──────────────────────────────────┐
        │   Arrange guarantee and mortgage  │
        └──────────────────────────────────┘
                        │
          ┌──────────────────────────────┐
          │    Find and purchase land     │
          └──────────────────────────────┘
                        │
          ┌──────────────────────────────┐
          │    Seek planning permission   │
          └──────────────────────────────┘
                        │
    ┌──────────────────────────────────────┐
    │  Appoint a contractor or subcontractors │
    └──────────────────────────────────────┘
                        │
┌────────────────────────────────────────────────────────────────┐
│ Manage the building work and specify materials (if using subcontractors) │
└────────────────────────────────────────────────────────────────┘
```

FINDING A PLOT OF LAND

This is often the slowest but most expensive part of the whole project. The average price of a plot is around £35,000 to £45,000 for a ¼ acre plot (enough for a three- to four-bedroom house), but land is available for as little as £7,000 to £10,000 in areas such as Wales.

Where to look

Local newspapers and magazines Check local papers under Land for Sale in the classified section. Advertising that you are looking for land is often a good idea. Specialist self-build magazines are a good source of adverts for land.

New towns and local authorities Some new towns around the country set aside particular areas for self-build or have plots available between existing developments, known as infill plots. These have the advantage of secured planning permission and are often serviced plots, i.e. they have vital services such as water and electricity laid on. Contact the CNT (Commission for New Towns).

Local authorities may also sell serviced plots. It's worth enquiring if there are any sites with buildings due for demolition that may be suitable.

Land-search companies There are companies specialising in finding land for prospective house-builders. Landbank Services (registration fee £27) and the National Land Finding Agency (registration fee just under £29) offer nationwide land searches.

If you are looking in a particular area, contact a local land-search company (look out for adverts in specialist magazines).

Local agents and professionals Many of the major estate agents will help find land. Local architects and builders may be able to point you in the right direction for finding sites in the area. Many companies offering self-build packages can also help find land.

The size of the plot

Decide on the size of house you are aiming for so that you can consider, realistically, the size of the plot. You may need to be flexible with your plans to suit the land available. As a guide, add at least 1m (just over 3ft) at each side, 8m (26ft) at the front and 10m (33ft) at the rear of your plan to give the rough size of land plot you will need. This equates to about 1,000 sq m (¼ acre) for a three- to four-bedroom house.

Planning Permission

Outline planning permission (OPP) Planning permission for a development has been agreed in principle by the local authority. You will need to apply for detailed planning permission before any building can take place. Outline planning permission is valid for three years, so check when the consent runs out before progressing with an offer to buy. If it has only one year left, you will have difficulty securing finance from a bank or building society.

Detailed planning permission (DPP) Consent is given to build a particular dwelling, including the plans and the final appearance. If a plot has DPP, check that the plan drawings are included in the price of the land and that you will be able to use them. DPP is valid for five years. Planning permission belongs to the land and is transferred with the change in ownership.

You can apply for planning permission on land you do not own, which is often done by prospective purchasers, but you have a legal obligation to tell the owner about the application.

Remember Beware of plots often advertised as 'potential plot' as this means they have no planning permission. Don't buy any land before outline planning permission (sometimes referred to as planning consent) has been given by the local planning office. Be sure to check for any conditions attached to the permission. Contact your local council for further details about planning permission. Always employ a solicitor to carry out conveyancing, including searches, before progressing with the purchase

Factors to take into account

When considering a plot of land, stand back and think about a few points:
- Why has no one built on the land before? It may be simply that the land has only just become available – or it could have adverse features such as a high risk of flooding.
- Are water, electricity and drainage available?

- Is the site accessible from an existing road, or will you have to make arrangements to cross someone else's land?
- Does the surface look well drained?
- Are there any mature trees that could interfere with your plans? Some trees are covered by preservation orders.
- Is there evidence of any obstructions that would be expensive to move, such as old foundations?

Remember When considering a plot of land, bear in mind factors you would look at if buying a house. How far is it from shops and local services? Is the site close to noisy roads (*see* Chapter 2, House-hunting). You will also need a conveyancer to carry out the legal stages of buying the land and transferring the ownership. He may wish to use a surveyor or structural engineer to check that the site is suitable for building on.

Land can sometimes be sold by auction and follows the same principles as buying a house at auction (for details *see* Other Ways of Buying Property, page 22).

PROJECT MANAGEMENT METHODS

Although there are many circumstances that determine how you organise your self-build, there are two main options: employing subcontractors and managing the project yourself, or employing a self-build property company.

Managing the project yourself

This is a popular method, with around 30 per cent of self-build projects managed by the individual. The greatest savings can be made with this method of building. However, you will have to make time available to monitor the build, and you will need good organisation skills to ensure things run smoothly and to schedule.

This approach gives you greater flexibility of design and materials. You will need to employ an architect to assist in the planning and acquisition of building consent, but are then left to manage the build yourself, sourcing your own subcontractors. It is an advantage to use contractors experienced in self-build projects. They know the way things should run, which should give you greater confidence in the project.

Remember Obtain at least three quotes and ask to see previous projects before securing a contractor.

The Associated Self Build Architects have members across the country, all of whom are member architects of the Royal Institute of British Architects and particularly experienced in self-build projects. They will also be familiar with local availability of land, realistic prices, planning applications and procedures, and local building regulations.

You can use an architect simply for the initial stages of the design, which will cost you about £2,000. Alternatively, an architect can carry out the designing and manage the project for you, organising planning and contractors, which costs between 6 and 13 per cent of the building cost.

Your architect should also be able to give you Architect's Certificates at different stages of the project (*see* Structural Guarantees, pages 101–3).

The more you are prepared to take on, the greater the potential savings, but you will have to cost out your own time. There is no strict rule for the option you take and how much you are involved – it will depend upon your circumstances and experience. If you have experience with the building industry you may already have sufficient contacts. If you're starting from scratch you will appreciate having someone at hand who knows the ropes and can make considered arrangements for you.

Organising the build yourself and employing contractors directly cuts out the middle men who each add their own mark-up and ultimately increase the overall cost.

Using a self-build property company

Using a package company should simplify the whole process. There are plenty of self-build companies offering self-build packages. Check whether the companies offer complete 'turnkey' packages, managing the whole project, or just offer a design service and supply materials.

GUIDE TO COSTS		
Method of project management	Per sq m	Per sq ft
Self-managed, with extensive DIY involvement	£323-£388	£30-£36
Entire project completed by single contractor	£430-£484	£40-£45
Self-build package, turnkey project	£484-£646	£45-£60
Complete project managed by architect	£560-£667	£52-£62

The prices in the table are a general guide. Your own costs will be strongly governed by your final specifications and the building materials and fittings used. Whichever route you take to build your house, you will have to decide which construction method to use for the basic structure.

Construction methods

There are two main methods of construction: timber-framed or brick-and -block construction. Most companies only offer one so your choice of company may depend upon which method you prefer. Companies such as Investment Homes offer either method of construction.

Despite the different structures, the final appearance is identical, and insurance companies make no distinction between the two types of construction.

Timber-framed houses Timber-framed house building has been a traditional method for many centuries, with the Tudor style of building the best-known of these structures. The timber frame forms the supporting structure. The interior is lined with plasterboard, and externally, protective cladding, usually brick, is used.

Around 45 per cent of self-build houses are timber-framed. The main advantage is the short construction time. A waterproof shell can be completed within about two weeks, facilitating work on the interior whilst the outside brickwork cladding is built around the shell. It also gives a very energy-efficient structure.

Brick-and-block house A brick-and-block house is constructed with solid masonry exterior walls. This is the most popular building method in the construction industry as a whole, but it does involve greater manpower in construction.

A method of building recently introduced from Germany consists of interlocking polystyrene blocks which are filled and secured with a core of concrete. This method affords a high level of thermal insulation. The walls are finished inside with plasterboard and on the outside with rendering. The advantages include very fast construction of the house shell. Although the construction materials are more expensive this is offset by the lower labour cost and rapid progress.

SELECTING A SELF-BUILD COMPANY

Self-build companies are brimming with literature to help you through the minefield of information and options, but are essentially tempting you to take up their services.

Many encourage you to visit sites. For example, Potton have a purpose-built Self-build Sales Centre (at St Neots, Cambridgeshire) where you see houses and speak to their sales staff. Self-build seminars are also held at their headquarters (in Sandy, Bedfordshire).

It is advisable to visit sites of previous customers to get a feel for what's on offer, but try to leave this until you have more confirmed ideas, otherwise too much information will cloud your thoughts.

Different companies offer different packages. Some only design and supply, while others provide a full package of design, supply and build.

The designs also vary. Most companies have a choice of basic, standard house plans which can be modified to your requirements. Even if you choose a standard design, the appearance of the house can vary considerably depending upon the finish you use. You could use tiles or slates, timber trim or brick.

Package companies have a range of basic plans, but start with your own

Same plan, different look.
Potton's Gransden with
various cladding finishes.

ideas based on the site's features and plans can be tailor-made to suit you.
Computer-aided design is often used.

Most companies will adapt to your individual project procedure,
offering to provide part of the package, such as handing over to local
subcontractors, or, alternatively, a complete turnkey project (managing the
complete project including the subcontractors and materials).

Comparing costs

Most companies quote a cost per square metre or square foot as a guideline
but check exactly what this includes before using it as a comparison
between companies. Quotes per square metre/foot usually apply to the
actual floor area living space and exclude garage and loft space.

Remember Don't forget to check what the figure for a self-build package
on the bottom line relates to. For example, does it include decoration,
kitchen units and other features?

The main costs come from the labour and materials. The more people
there are involved in the project, the more the price increases, each person
adding their own mark-up. If the main contractor employs a
subcontractor who himself employs additional labour, the cost will be

Examples of self-build companies

Prices and times vary and should be used as a guide only. These companies are given only as examples.

Timber-framed

● BORDER OAK specialise in building half-timbered houses using traditional 16th-century construction methods and materials combined with modern technology. It takes two to four weeks to complete the frame on site, after eight to ten weeks sourcing suitable oak and preparing it in the workshop. The complete build takes about six months. A three-bedroom cottage of about 132 sq m/1,420 sq ft, costs about £641.50 per sq m/£59.60 per sq ft, for a total cost of £84,635 excluding land.

● HOSBY SALE LTD build Danish-style houses using Danish materials. The foundations and main shell take about six weeks, with the average build taking 16 weeks. Costs start at around £484 per sq m/£45 per sq ft.

● BERGHUS use Scandinavian technology but the components are manufactured in Cornwall to meet individuals' specifications. Construction is rapid, and basic erection within as little as a week, before external cladding is built. Costs are in the region of £484 per sq m/£45 per sq ft for a complete 'turnkey' package. The complete building process takes about three months.

● POTTON LTD offer the design and materials only, but have a large selection of builders experienced in constructing their houses. Their contract manager will oversee the project but you employ the subcontractors. It has been known for a Potton timber-framed house to be completed in a record time of 33 days, but the usual build schedule is 15 to 20 weeks. Using subcontracted labour you are looking at about £409 per sq m/£38 per sq ft.

Brick-and-block

● A company offering a brick-and-block package is DESIGN AND MATERIALS. Their complete build takes about four to five months, at a cost of about £430-£538 per sq m/£40-£50 per sq ft.

● BECO PRODUCTS offer Wallform construction using polystyrene blocks. Construction of the basic shell takes about six days. For a three-bedroom house the cost of the shell would be around £5,500 excluding labour. You have to organise the completion of the build.

greater than using one local labourer.

Building costs can vary from £323 to £700 per square metre/£30 to £65 per square foot; as a guideline the average is about £484 per square metre/£45 per square foot, including everything except the land.

Remember Before signing up with a company ask to visit previous projects. The company should be willing to give you names and addresses of clients. Visit them and ask their opinion of the company: Were the quoted costs realistic in the end? Was the workmanship satisfactory? Were there any major problems? Was the project completed within the time scale agreed?

FINANCE

You will need money to finance the purchase of land and other costs such as planning permission, architect's fees and legal costs.

Self-build companies require a deposit followed by payment at each significant step of the construction. The lender will check that each stage of the construction is to their satisfaction before releasing any money.

There are also costs to be taken into account that would come up with a normal house purchase, such as employing a conveyancer.

Planning permission for a new house will cost at least £160.

Stamp Duty will be payable on land over £60,000 in the same way as when you are purchasing an existing house.

Your conveyancer will also charge for his services and for registration with the Land Registry (*see* Costs of Moving House, pages 11-17).

A Guide to Sizes

The quoted size relates to the actual square metrage/footage of living area, i.e. the internal floor area. Remember that 1 sq m = 10.76 sq ft.

A three-bedroom detached house = 93 sq m/1,000 sq ft.

A four-bedroom house with two bathrooms = 150 sq m/1,600 sq ft.

When looking at land, remember to add space front and back, and each side.

Progress mortgages

Most banks and building societies will arrange mortgages for self-build clients. Although finance brokers can shop around for mortgage plans to suit your circumstances, a progress mortgage is the usual type of loan, releasing money at specific stages of the build. Bradford & Bingley is the largest lender to self-builders and are a good source of information. Progress mortgages vary from lender to lender. Different percentages of the loan are allocated for the different stages, such as land purchase and construction stages. Check with the lender and the company building the house if using a package company; you may need to negotiate to suit both parties.

Before confirming a mortgage, your lender will need to see evidence that the project is a sound investment. He will expect documentation, from your conveyancer, that the land is suitable and has all the necessary planning consents.

To ensure a sound structure you must be able to provide details of your builder and any schemes you are planning to guarantee the work, such as signing up for the Buildmark or Custom Build Warranty, or an Architect's Certificate (*see* Structural Guarantees, pages 101-3).

The lender will expect the house to be completed within 12 months.

After completion you will need to convert your progress mortgage into a conventional mortgage. You will be able to apply for any of the usual house-buyer mortgages (*see* Chapter 4, Arranging a Mortgage).

Insurance for the mortgage

When you take out a progress mortgage it works rather like an endowment mortgage in that you only pay the interest on the debt. You will need to take out or review your life insurance to make sure the debt will be repaid if you die before completion.

Insurance for the build

You'll need to organise this yourself. It rarely exceeds about 0.7 per cent of the overall project cost and is worth taking out to avoid unnecessary expense should something go wrong. The types you will need are as follows:

Public liability insurance To cover injuries to the public or their property as a consequence of your building operations, such as passing cars damaged by materials left on the road, or someone else's electricity cable being cut by accident.

Employer's liability insurance A legal requirement if you are employing anyone, including subcontractors, on your site.

General site and building insurance To cover any damage to the property during construction, such as theft of materials, vandalism or weather damage.

DMS Services offer a comprehensive package for self-builders through the Norwich Union.

STRUCTURAL GUARANTEES

Structural guarantees are essential if you are to secure finance from a lender. They will also make the property easier to sell, as they tell the buyer that the house was well built in the first place. If the property has no guarantee, any potential purchasers will have difficulty securing a mortgage.

If any structural alterations are undertaken while the property is still under guarantee, you should check that the guarantee is not invalidated.

There are three guarantees you can use which cover the house against any structural problems:

National House-building Council

Most builders or developers are members of the NHBC. All the work is done by an NHBC-registered builder and is checked by inspectors during its course so that it qualifies for a NHBC Certificate, know as the Buildmark Warranty. The same warranty is used for new house building. It provides ten years' insurance cover. The first two cover you against the builder not completing the work and any defects arising from the builder not adhering to NHBC technical standards. For the final eight years you are covered against actual major structural damage.

If the NHBC-registered builder completes only the shell of the house, this is all that will be covered by the Buildmark; any subcontractors' work will not be covered. To cover the cost of NHBC inspection services and provision of the warranty, about $1^{1}/_{2}$ per cent of the final estimated value of the property is paid to your builder.

Zurich Municipal

The Custom Build Guarantee is more appropriate if you want to manage the construction and be more involved. It runs for ten years but may be extended to 15.

The construction has to be carried out in accordance with the Zurich technical manual and the work checked at critical stages by a Custom Build surveyor.

You are less restricted by who carries out the work than with the Buildmark Warranty, as long as it meets the requirements of the surveyors. As an alternative to using a Zurich-registered builder to build the house complete, Custom Build allows the option of appointing the subcontractors directly. All aspects of the construction are covered, not just the 'shell'.

Costs of using the Custom Build scheme vary. As an example, it would cost around £900 for a house of about 150 sq m/1,600 sq ft.

Architect's Certificate

An Architect's Inspection Certificate shows that an architect has been involved professionally in the building of the property, and that the house has been built to a good professional quality. You will have recourse against the architect should anything fail to perform as expected.

An architect offering certificates must have professional indemnity insurance for the certificate to be accepted by a lender.

A series of visits are normally made during the key stages of the construction and you will be charged between £40 and £100 per visit.

Claiming back VAT

VAT is not paid on any new housing so any VAT you pay during the course of building the house and buying materials can be claimed back. If you deal with a package company who erect some of the building for you, they will not charge VAT.

If you choose to use your own subcontractors for any of the build, they should not charge you any VAT, but remember to check whether VAT can be claimed for any materials purchased.

The claiming process can sometimes prove complicated, as you can claim for some items but not others. For example, you can claim back VAT on an Aga or Rayburn because it is a permanent fixture but cannot claim it on a built-in cooker. Generally, if you can take a fitting with you if you move, you cannot claim VAT.

Claims have to be made within three months of completion, and only one application can be made.

You can't claim back VAT on any later additions, for example a conservatory or extra garage. It may be more economical to include these in the initial build.

It's a good idea to contact your local Customs and Excise office and read through the forms before you embark on the project. It is easier if you know what information will be needed when you come to fill in the forms at the end and can record details and receipts correctly as you go along.

For further details a leaflet, 'VAT refunds for do-it-yourself builders', is available from your local Customs and Excise office.

CHAPTER 7

Selling Your Home

Using an estate agent is the most popular way of selling a property, but you may opt for selling it yourself or selling by auction.

ESTATE AGENTS AND CONVEYANCERS

Estate agents

For advice on choosing an estate agent, *see* Chapter 3, Using the Professionals. Ask for quotes from at least three estate agents before instructing one or more of them. The fee is normally based on the selling price of the house and is between 1 and 3 per cent of the final selling price.

As a guide, 2 per cent of a selling price of £66,000 is £1,320. It is worth trying to negotiate the fee. Some agents offer a flat fee while others will offer a cheaper deal if they are sole agents (see page 52).

Remember VAT ($17^1/_2$ per cent) will be added to any fees charged by an estate agent.

Ensure that you check what is included in a quote from an agent. Will you have to pay for extra advertising? Is a withdrawal fee quoted?

If you're considering additional specialist advertising, confirm the costs (sometimes quoted per centimetre or per advert) at the outset before agreeing to anything. How often will an agent put your property in the local paper? Different agents put different priorities on using advertising, and some will include the costs in a fixed price.

On occasion, estate agents may approach you offering to sell your house, particularly if there has been a lot of interest in similar houses in

The best time of year to sell

The property market does vary across the country but generally there are peaks and troughs in the market, except in London which doesn't really follow a trend.

Autumn and spring are generally the best times to put a house on the market. September is often a 'new start' time of year associated with returning to school. Buyers want to get settled before Christmas and the depths of winter. Houses also look attractive with autumn colour at this time, before all the leaves fall and places begin to look bleak and cold. Christmas is a quiet time of year but there may be a few buyers around looking for bargains.

Early spring is a good time to put a property on the market, before the market gets too saturated with sellers. As spring makes way for summer the market will begin to quieten again. Buyers become distracted by summer holidays, but like Christmas there may be a few bargain hunters around.

your road. Check the deal that the estate agent is offering you; even though you were approached you will have to pay a fee. If you are already selling through another agent, consider the terms and your contract carefully in order to avoid paying two commissions.

Conveyancers

You will need a conveyancer to deal with the legal side of selling your home, for example drawing up and agreeing contracts. For advice in this, *see* Chapter 3, Using the Professionals.

DIY SELLING

If you want to save the cost of instructing an agent to sell your house, you could have a go at selling it yourself. Around 5 per cent of homes in the UK are sold privately.

Setting the price

To get an idea of how much to ask for your house, see how much similar properties in the area are selling for.

If this proves difficult, have a professional valuation. (See Yellow pages under surveyors and valuers or contact the Royal Institution of Chartered Surveyors or Incorporated Society of Valuers and Auctioneers for local members.)

A valuation report will assess only that, so you might also consider having a structural survey to find out the condition of the property before setting a price (*see* Chapter 2, House-hunting). Valuation reports cost between £70 and £150.

Compiling the sales particulars

Put together the sales particulars in the same way as an estate agent would. Buyers will be used to this format.

It's advisable to put a disclaimer on your details such as 'these particulars are believed to be accurate and are set out as a general outline only for the guidance of interested buyers. They do not constitute, nor constitute part of, an offer or contract.'

Recognised abbreviations for describing property	
CH	central heating
CHW	constant hot water
wc	loo
clk	cloakroom
gge	garage
rm	room
Repl. D/G	replacement double glazing
f/f kit	fully fitted kitchen
exc.con	excellent condition
c&c	carpets and curtains
lge	large
f&f	fixtures and fittings
det	detached
o.n.o	or near offer
kit/brkrm	kitchen/breakfast room
conv.	converted
FH	freehold
GR	ground rent

Be accurate with the details – you don't want to leave yourself open to damages through misrepresentation.

Advertising

It's a good idea to set yourself a budget for advertising, so that you don't start eating into the savings from not using an estate agent.

Local newspapers often have good property sections and are one of the places buyers will browse through when sounding out a local market. You could try regional or national newspapers, or even property publications, but these can prove expensive. They should only be considered if you have something special to offer.

Putting up a sign gives an instant invitation to view. The number and size of signs are regulated by the local authority. Check with their planning department first, as the regulations vary for different areas.

Showing people around

Interested parties may call directly after seeing your 'for sale' sign. You may be open to nosy buyers who are just looking because you are advertising, since they do not have the hassle of formally going through an estate agent.

Remember You may be keen to have as many viewers as possible, but bear security in mind. Be cautious – try to avoid letting strangers in if you're on your own.

Always take down a name and address, and ask for identity if in doubt.

Once a buyer has been found and the price agreed, the rest of the selling process is normally handed over to your solicitor or licensed conveyancer.

Be prepared to negotiate the price and conditions personally, as houses rarely sell at the original asking price.

APPEALING TO POTENTIAL BUYERS

Estate agents usually offer to show potential buyers around but it is advisable for you to be there at the time. You are the ideal person to show off the best bits and answer any relevant questions about the property.

You will have to put time aside for this and should instruct your estate agent to arrange weekend and evening viewing if this is more convenient.

Sometimes there will be a case where a buyer wants to look at a property when you know you will not be around. Arrange to have a key left with the estate agent with the assurance that a representative will accompany the buyer.

There are many well-known tips for making your house seem inviting, such as fresh flowers and the aroma of freshly brewed coffee, but on a more serious note there are some important points to attend to:

- Replace blown light bulbs and mend dripping taps.
- Repair sashcords and replace missing door knobs and broken slates.
- Clear and tidy away clutter, especially from the hallway and staircase, which create the first impression.
- Bathrooms and kitchens are often scrutinised, so keep them clean and tidy.
- Clean windows.
- Tidy the garden including cutting the lawn and weeding the beds.
- Keep the access clear, trim back overhanging plants and clear snow in the winter.
- Make sure the house number or name is easily identifiable and that your doorbell works.
- Keep pets out of the way and children quiet.
- Music or the TV can be distracting.
- After the guided tour invite questions and then let the prospective buyer have a further look in their own time.

To redecorate or not?

It's a good idea to touch up any flaking paint or loose wallpaper, but a complete recent redecoration can cause suspicion. Buyers may think you are covering problems like damp patches or cracked walls.

If you do feel you need to put a few fresh licks of paint around the place choose relatively neutral warm colours.

AFTER THE OFFER

Any interested buyers will make an offer 'subject to contract'. They will instruct a surveyor to assess your house. He will need to visit during the daytime while it is light.

If the survey is simply a valuation report it will take only about 15 minutes, but structural surveys take longer, even up to several hours. When an appointment is made, ask how long it will take so that you can make arrangements; you may need to take an afternoon off work.

If anything doubtful comes to light, such as the condition of timbers or possible damp, appointments for specialist surveyors may also need to be made.

If the buyer is satisfied with the conveyancing they will proceed with a confirmed offer. At this stage you will probably have to negotiate your price. When the housing market is quiet, buyers will try to buy at a lower price because they know the seller is probably keen to sell.

Once an offer has been agreed you can feel a bit more confident about arranging to buy a new property for yourself. It then can become rather a juggling act to co-ordinate both your sale and the purchase of a new house.

At the exchange of contracts your buyer will pay a deposit which makes the buy–sell arrangement legal and binding. A completion date will need to be arranged which will have to match with moving into your new property, as you must give vacant possession to the buyer on the completion date.

Try to arrange the completion for your new house before the completion date with your buyer so that you have a few days to move into your new house. You may want to have access to the new house to give it a thorough clean before unloading your furniture and this also offers a slightly more leisurely opportunity to clean your old house after the furniture has been removed.

Make the surveyor's job easier:

- Unlock doors and window
- Clear the access to the loft
- Make sure the garage is open
- Supply a step ladder
- Put the central heating on in the winter

SELLING BY AUCTION

Selling by auction can be a fast way to sell your house so you should ideally have made provision for new accommodation and storage for furniture if necessary.

A date for completion is set before the auction, usually four weeks after. This is included in the selling guide.

Properties are usually sold by auction in order to obtain the highest market price (executors usually use this method when dealing with estates of the deceased). An auction is also a good method if it is otherwise difficult to put a value on a property, for example if the property is unusual, as the market finds the best price.

The cost of selling by auction

Auctioneers' fees are along the lines of those charged by estate agents – in the region of 1 to 3 per cent, but on top of this you will have to pay the preparation costs. The auctioneer will prepare a brochure and probably special advertising which you will be expected to pay for. The use of the auction room is an additional cost, but you could make a saving if the auction includes a selection of properties.

A solicitor will be needed to carry out the legal work for you.

The auctioneer usually sends the payment to your solicitor, who, after deducting any charges, will pay you the remainder accompanied by a full statement.

Remember You will have to pay auction costs even if the property doesn't sell.

Consulting an auctioneer

You should consult only a qualified property auctioneer as anyone can organise an auction without a qualification. The Incorporated Society of Valuers and Auctioneers can give you details of local firms in your area.

The auctioneer will advise whether or not the property is suitable for sale by auction. As with all contracts you should confirm the costs and details at the outset. You will then agree the possible auction date, what is to be included and the viewing arrangements. Your auctioneer will propose a sale guide price and a reserve price, below which offers will not be accepted.

The auction

The aim is obviously to exceed the asking price but if you do not even reach the reserve price you can still sell privately to an interested party, possibly immediately after the auction.

If the auction is successful the auctioneer signs the contract on your behalf and receives the 10 per cent deposit. The remaining balance is usually required within 28 days, but this detail should be specified in the contract drawn up beforehand.

CHAPTER 8

Moving Home

The actual process of moving can be very stressful and often physically tiring. Organisation is essential for a smooth, trouble-free move.

If you opt for the full services of a removals firm they can take on the majority of the work including packing and unpacking, transportation, insurance, storage if necessary, and even cleaning services on occasion.

INITIAL DECISIONS

Start planning the actual move as far ahead as you can, to make sure you aren't forced by circumstances to move on a day that is inconvenient, or to use a removals firm you are not happy with.

What day to move

Have some idea of when you want to move before you exchange contracts so you can discuss a completion date with your buyer. If you build in some time between the completion of your purchase and the sale of your old home it will give you greater flexibility to decide on which day you actually move.

Weekends, particularly at the end of the month, are the most popular time to move. Bank holidays and school holidays are also popular moving times.

If you can avoid peak periods you may be able to negotiate discounts with removals firms.

Doing it yourself

This is only recommended if you are moving locally, have relatively few possessions and have the time and energy to arrange it. You will have to enlist the help of friends or family.

If you are planning to move over a weekend bear in mind that there will be greater demand for hire vehicles so book well in advance.

Calculate how many loads you will make up and how long you need the vehicle for. Remember that you will probably have to return it at the end of the move.

Make sure all your packing is done well in advance. You'll need to arrange your own packing boxes, ropes or webbing for securing items, and blankets or other packing for protecting furniture.

Weigh up the pros and cons before deciding on a DIY removal. What may first appear a cheap option can take a great deal of time and include less obvious costs. You may need to use a lot of petrol, and provide meals for your 'movers'. Also check that you, personally, are adequately insured against physical injury.

Hiring a Vehicle

- Choose a hire company that is a member of the British Vehicle Rental and Leasing Association, which sets quality of service standards.
- You can drive up to a $7^1/_2$ tonne van on your standard driving licence if you passed your test before April 1995. The limit for new standard driving licences is now a $3^1/_2$ tonne vehicle. If you think you will need a larger van, it may be worth finding someone to drive who has an older licence.
- A vehicle with a tail lift makes loading a lot easier but it adds to the weight of the vehicle and so reduces the size that you can hire.
- Drivers usually have to be over 25 years old and have a clean driving licence (some minor convictions may be disregarded).
- The costs vary between dealers. Always read the conditions and check what is included in the charge before using a company.
- Expect to pay around £75 for a day, and be prepared to pay a large deposit.
- Insurance cover varies too; some companies offer cover against collision and theft but not overhead damage, while others may offer cover against only one type of damage or loss. For a small fee you can reduce the damage excess (how much you have to pay before the company pays for any damage).

On the Move

Ryder specialise in providing help for the DIY remover. Their Home Move Packs include items such as packing boxes, cartons, tape and rope and cost from £39.50, or you can buy any amount of different packaging items, such as mattress covers and portable wardrobe boxes. You can hire a hand truck for trolleying heavy items, and furniture blankets for protecting of your belongings. Different size vehicles can be hired to suit your needs and you can choose 'One Way Rental' which means you leave it at the Ryder location nearest to your new home. The hire cost of a 3.7 metre/12 foot box van, enough for an average two-bedroom house, is around £45 (including collision damage waiver and personal accident insurance) plus a £100 refundable deposit.

In the long run it may be less stressful to hand the job over to a professional firm.

Hiring a removals firm

Once you have an idea of when you want to move and the services you need, approach at least three removals companies for quotes. Ask friends and relatives if they have any recommendations, or your local estate agent may well be able to suggest a company.

Choose a removals company who is a member of the British Association of Removers (BAR). Local firms will advertise in the Yellow Pages or local papers, or you can contact BAR for details of members.

Firms will send someone around to assess the size of the move and estimate the cost. Beforehand, make a list of things to include.

Take the following into consideration:

- Are fitted carpets to be lifted? Removers will often lift carpets but not refit them at the other end.
- Remember to check what is in the loft, shed and garage. Quotes are higher if there is a loft or garage full of things.
- You should point out anything that needs special handling, for example old paintings or a vintage wine collection. Also tell them

what to expect in terms of access to the new home. Most major removals firms are used to moving delicate items such as pianos and clocks, and if there are exceptional circumstances they can contract a specialist mover to help.

- If you are taking a freezer, will it need to be emptied and switched off beforehand?
- When you accept an estimate you will also have to confirm the date. As a back-up put everything in writing including any special arrangements or articles requiring careful handling. Keep a copy yourself.

Remember Check what each quote includes. For example, packing may be extra. Do you have to pay overtime for long moves? Does the price include VAT?

INSURANCE

Household insurance for your new house should be arranged to start from the date contracts are exchanged.

You will also need to insure your house contents during the move. Some removals firms will offer insurance to cover the move; alternatively you can arrange cover on your household policy. Check which offers you the most comprehensive cover and acceptable price.

House insurance doesn't automatically cover removals, so you will need to arrange to extend the policy.

The British Association of Removers offers a Careline Guarantee which provides up to £1,500 worth of protection against anything going wrong with the move, your car or even emergencies at your new home during the first three months of occupancy.

Insurance through the removals firm may specify certain conditions. They do not generally accept responsibility for damaged items unless they packed and unpacked the items themselves. You normally have to make any claims within a certain time, which can be as little as three days after the move.

Factors affecting removals costs

- Number and type of belongings.
- Whether there is a loft or garage to empty.
- Access at the old and new properties.
- Whether they are packing and lifting carpets.
- If you are willing to share space in the lorry. Sometimes the other half of a lorry will be used to transport someone else's things, but you can request not to share a lorry.
- Day of move. Popular days, such as weekends, increase the price, but it depends upon demand.
- Distance does not increase the costs considerably, as the majority of the fee is for the manpower.

Insurers will normally include a 'pairs and set clause': they will not pay for the cost of replacing any undamaged remainder of a set, such as glasses or a dinner service, if one item is broken and a replacement can't be found.

COST OF REMOVALS

Quotes from different firms will vary depending upon whether you are using a national firm or smaller local one. Different parts of the country also affect the price; it is often more expensive if you are moving within an urban area. Expect to pay from at least £300 for a good company.

If the firm is packing and unpacking for you, the move may take two days. For example, a two-day local move (packing and unpacking) for a three-bedroom house without insurance could cost around £650.

PUTTING ITEMS INTO STORAGE

If you are not moving into your new home straight away or you are temporarily moving into a smaller property, you might consider putting some items into storage with a removals firm.

Most major removals firms offer storage facilities; contact the British Association of Removers for details.

Shop around, asking for quotes from three companies.

Stored items are usually packed into sealed containers, commonly 7 cubic metres/250 cubic feet, which are unloaded at the depot and left unopened until you need them again. It's a good idea to put some thought into what to store.

Storage is quoted as a specific cubic capacity for a period of time. Payment is usually quarterly in advance, but you can store items for shorter periods.

Remember A charge will be made if you need access to your possessions. If you know you will need something in the future, for example next season's clothes, make sure that it is labelled 'keep forward' so that the packers can put them at the front.

Costs of storage

Storage costs also vary considerably depending upon the company and the way they quote. Most charge a cost by volume used but may charge by the week or month. They usually expect some payment in advance.

Remember When considering quotes, check whether they include VAT and insurance. Insurance can be arranged by the storage firm or special arrangements can be made under your house contents insurance.

How much do you own?

Calculate how much space your possessions will take up using the guide sizes on page 118. You can use this information for calculating storage costs. For example, for all the items listed overleaf, which total 11.8 cubic metres/418 cubic feet, you'd need two of the standard 7 cubic metre/250 cubic foot containers. It is

Clean-sheet Approach

If you are putting carpets, blankets or clothes into storage, make sure that they are thoroughly cleaned to prevent problems from moth damage. Carpet cleaning should be done in good time to make sure they dry out completely otherwise they could suffer from mildew growth.

Item	Cubic feet per item	Cubic meters per item
3-seater sofa	35	0.99
book case	12	0.34
breakfast table	10	0.28
sideboard	25	0.71
dining chair	4	0.11
occasional chair	14	0.40
desk	20	0.57
foot stool	2	0.06
mirror	3	0.08
rugs	8	0.23
standard lamp	3	0.08
coffee table	4	0.11
television	18	0.51
hi-fi	12	0.34
chest of drawers	20	0.57
double bed	45	1.27
single bed	30	0.85
wardrobe	36	1.02
cooker	25	0.71
washing machine	20	0.57
high chair	3	0.08
fridge	30	0.85
vacuum cleaner	3	0.08
linen basket	3	0.08
filing cabinet	8	0.21
garden chair	3	0.08
lawn mower	5	0.14
step ladder	5	0.14
wheelbarrow	6	0.17
bicycle	6	0.17

also useful for making sure you have a suitable sized vehicle if you are doing the move yourself.

SORTING OUT YOUR POSSESSIONS

Moving house is probably the only time when you have a really good sort-out and get right to the back of the cupboards and into the loft. There will inevitably be a lot of things to get rid off, especially if you have been in one place for some time and the children have now grown up. Set yourself up with three large bin bags labelled 'Rubbish', 'Charity' and 'Sell'. Many removal firms can provide bags and boxes destined for Oxfam.

ANTIQUE VALUATION

If you have items that may be worth a lot, for example antiques, it's a good idea to have them valued properly, whether it's to sell now or to arrange adequate insurance cover when you move.

Disposing of rubbish

Contact your local authority for details about your nearest tip. They usually have recycling facilities for paper and metal and sometimes plastic. If you have a lot of rubbish you could hire a skip (see box).

In the process of clearing out the shed or garage, you may come across old cans of paint or oil, or other flammable or toxic chemicals. These should be disposed of safely using council facilities at a local tip. They should never be poured down the drain or put in the dustbin.

Take old medicines or pills back to the doctor or chemist.

Hiring a Skip

The usual size of a skip for house rubbish is between 4 and 6 cu yds. Costs vary from region to region because the cost of disposing of the rubbish varies.

Expect to pay around £65, different companies charge a small fee on top per day or the fee may be fixed for say one week.

If the skip will be on the road you need a permit from your local authority (highways department), which is usually free unless you are using a parking bay.

If the skip is on the road you will need to have lamps, which can usually be hired from the skip company, for around an extra £15.

Giving it away

Take jumble to local charity shops. Your local authority should have details of local charities or other needy concerns or voluntary organisations. Some will even come and collect large items such as furniture. Local schools or play groups will probably be grateful for any toys or books.

Selling

Car boot sales have become very popular and there's bound to be one in your area. Check local newspapers for forthcoming sales and contact the organiser beforehand. It's usually cheaper to book a car in in advance.

You could try selling large items through the classified adverts in a local paper. Some secondhand shops will sell things for you on a sale-or-return basis and offer you a cut of the sale (see Curtain Exchanges, p 121).

PLANNING THE MOVE

Use the checklists given here to keep tabs on the arrangements for your move.

At least one month before

❏ **Service the car** You don't want any trouble in the middle of the move, particularly if you're moving to the other side of the country.

❏ **Schools in the new area** Arrange where your children will be transferred to. You may want to visit beforehand to meet the headteachers and weigh up the choices. Your new local authority can provide an information pack on schools in the area. For details of independent, fee-charging schools, contact the Independent Schools Information Service. Similarly the Pre-school Learning Alliance have a helpline for details of local groups. The Advisory Centre of Education (ACE) book, *School Choice and Appeals* (£4.50), provides details to consider when choosing a school. Other useful references include the *Good Nursery Guide* (£12.99) and the *Good State Schools Guide* (£12.99), both published by Vermilion.

Curtain exchanges

If the curtains won't fit your new house and you want to sell them, contact one of the curtain exchange agencies.

- The Curtain Exchange sell curtains for about a third the equivalent price when new; you will receive 60 per cent of the price they are sold for. There are about eleven agents covering the whole country.
- Hang-ups Curtain Re-sale Agency will sell curtains for you but keep 50 per cent of the sale price. There are about 15 agents across the country.

Curtain exchange agencies are a good source for buying quality curtains if you need them for your new home.

Home connections

❑ **Appliances** Book appropriate contractors you may need for disconnection at the old house and reconnection at the new. Local contractors can be found in the Yellow Pages or ask friends for recommendations. The Fair Trades Advisory Bureau has a register of vetted tradesmen, or contact the appropriate trade organisation mentioned below.

❑ **Gas man** Always use a Council for Registered Gas Installers (CORGI) registered contractor for dealing with gas appliances such as the cooker or checking the boiler at the new house.

❑ **Plumber** The Institute of Plumbing can provide details of local plumbers for disconnecting the washing machine and dishwasher. At the same time you could arrange for reconnection at the other end.

❑ **Electrician** For details of local electricians contact the National Inspection Council for Electrical Installation Contracting (NICEIC).

Contact the suppliers of services to your home and ask for a final reading. It's a good idea for you to note down the readings before you finally leave.

❑ **Electricity company**

❑ **Gas company**

❑ **Telephone company** Tell them about the move. It may be possible to take your current number with you if you are moving within the same telephone exchange area, or for an extra charge you can have the line transferred to your new home. Ask for the bill to be made up on the day of the move.

Contact the sellers of your new house and request that they don't have the services actually disconnected. It costs about £23 to have a line reconnected.

❑ **Water company** You may be entitled to a pro rata rebate on your water rates.

❑ **Redirection of mail** Use the form available from post offices, or phone the Royal Mail and book with a credit card (calls charged at local rate). Costs for mail redirection are: 1 month £6; 3 months £13; 1 year £30. You need to give at least one week's notice before you move. Parcelforce offer a redirection service for parcels; call 0800 224 466 for details.

❑ **TV licence** Take your old licence to a Post Office to have the address changed.

Rented goods
❑ **TV and video hire**
❑ **Washing machine hire**
Contact the rental company. You may be able to take them with you, otherwise arrange to return them. Make arrangements for hiring similar appliances at your new home if you need them.

Plan arrangements for the moving day
❑ **Children** If possible arrange for young children to stay with friends or

relatives. If this is not possible, organise something to occupy them such as colouring books or set them unpacking and exploring their new bedroom.

❏ **Pets** Although the removals firm will provide pet boxes for cats and sometimes dogs, consider putting them into kennels until you've organised yourself at the new home.

❏ **Overnight accommodation** If overnight accommodation is needed, book it well beforehand.

❏ **Hire of mobile phone** Hiring a mobile phone for the move often makes sense, especially if the phone is not connected at the new house. It means you can easily stay in touch with friends and relatives, and anyone else you might need to contact such as the electricity or gas companies, or your plumber.

The Carphone Warehouse (freephone 0800 424 800) offer mobile phones to hire from £7.95 a day, plus £1.00 a day insurance to cover loss, theft or damage, and charges 25p a unit to make calls.

For a fee, your telephone company will transfer any calls to your mobile phone but this is only feasible if you are taking your old phone number with you.

FINAL COUNTDOWN

Your organisation over the past few weeks (or more) should be starting to pay dividends, as the moving day approaches. Here is what you need to remember to do in those last hectic days.

Two weeks before
❏ Confirm date and time details with the remover.
❏ Cancel the milk and newspaper deliveries.
❏ Pick up any outstanding dry cleaning or shoe repairs.
❏ Return library books.
❏ Packing. Collect boxes, packing cases and newspaper for protection.

❑ Try to start packing at least two weeks before the move, unless the removers are doing it for you. Label the packages and boxes as you go, with the contents and which room they should go in at the other end.

❑ Start to send out address cards to friends and relatives with the date of your forthcoming move.

❑ Draw a floor plan of the new house – the removals firm can then put things in the right place when they arrive, furniture can be correctly positioned to save your moving it again.

❑ Start to prepare a 'moving survival kit' (see box).

❑ Run down your stocks of food especially in the freezer. It is best to transport an empty freezer; some removals firms will not take them with their contents and loss or damage to freezer contents is not usually covered by insurance.

Fridges and freezers should be handled with care to prevent damage to the cooling system; always carry them upright. At the other end, leave the freezer closed for as long as possible to let it settle to the correct temperature.

If it was emptied for the move, leave to stand, preferably overnight before switching it on again.

❑ Copy or draw a map of the route to the new house for the removals men.

Include phone numbers of both properties or your mobile phone so they can contact you if there are any hold-ups.

❑ Label any keys that you are leaving for the garage or shed.

The day before

❑ **Furniture** Dismantle any flat-pack furniture and remove any fixtures and fittings that are going with you, such as curtains.

❑ **Houseplants** Wrap in newspaper to protect them from draughts. At the other end they can stay wrapped until everything else is in and they have acclimatised. It's probably best to take them in the car with you, but remember not to leave them in a hot car in the summer.

❑ **Valuables and documents** Put these in a safe place. You may want to arrange safe keeping at the bank beforehand.

❏ Take pets to kennels or friends.

❏ Leave children with friends or relatives as arranged.

❏ Leave a contact phone number or address by the phone. The new owners can then inform anyone trying to contact you.

On the day

❏ Check everything is in the 'survival kit'.

Keep it close at hand so that it doesn't get packed in the removals lorry.

Moving Survival Kit

This should include all the essentials you are likely to need when you arrive. Take it with you in the car.

- kettle and mugs; plastic cups are lighter
- tea-bags / coffee
- milk (long life, powdered or individual portions)
- washing up bowl
- washing up liquid and other household cleaners
- rubber gloves
- toilet paper
- dustpan and brush
- bin liners
- light bulbs
- candles and matches
- plugs and fuses
- torch
- basic tools: screwdriver, pliers, adjustable spanner, hammer, nails and screws, tape, string.
- basic first aid kit, including plasters, painkillers and scissors
- easy snack food
- basic utensils; including tin opener and bottle opener
- note pad and pen
- money and credit cards
- self-sealing plug for sinks
- this book with useful phone numbers

You may not be able to finish packing it until you've finished plying the removals men with tea.

❑ **Food** Clear the kitchen of food, remembering the fridge and freezer.

❑ **Bedding** Strip the beds and put the bedding in a separate box ready for the first night at the other end. Include personal possessions you will also need for the first night as well as toiletries and towels.

❑ **Meter readings** Before you go take a final electricity and gas reading.

❑ **Keys** Collect the keys for the new house from your solicitor or estate agent, depending upon what has been arranged.

When the removals men arrive

❑ Explain the labelling on your packages and how it will relate to the plan at the new house.

❑ Point out any special arrangements that you have agreed. If they are doing the packing for you, give them plenty of space.

❑ Give them the map to the new house. Explain any details for parking they may need to know.

❑ Before you leave, have a final look around to check nothing has been overlooked.

❑ Switch off any appliances being left or the water supply as arranged with the new owner.

❑ Make sure there is someone at the other end, with the keys, to let the removals firm in and explain any arrangements to them.

Unloading at the new home

❑ Put the plan in each room. To ensure things are put in the right place.

❑ Take readings of the electricity and gas.

❑ Lay plastic sheeting or paper inside the door. This will save the carpets getting too soiled from people traipsing in and out.

❑ Switch the heating on if appropriate.

❑ Check that the lights work. Do this while there is still some daylight, if possible, so that you can see to change bulbs and fuses if necessary.

Once the removals men have finished

After the unloading and completion of the job, removals men normally expect a tip, usually about £5 per man.

If you have not been happy with the job, now is the time to say something. Put any comments on the discharge document that you will have to sign to confirm completion of the job.

Complaints are difficult to resolve after the event. Claims for removal damage must be made, in writing, usually within three days of the move. If you have not had a chance to unpack and check all your belongings, sign the discharge document 'unexamined'.

Unpacking

❏ Try to be systematical. Organise the beds ready to collapse into, while you've still got the energy.

❏ Hang curtains and unpack towels.

❏ Put any food in the fridge.

❏ You may want to clean the house before unpacking but be realistic as to what you can actually achieve before needing to unpack essentials. You will also tire very quickly if you try to do too much all at once.

Change of address

Who to inform about your change of address:

Services

You should contact them soon after the move to confirm the readings when you started to occupy the house:

❏ Electricity

❏ Gas

❏ Telephone

❏ Water

❏ Relatives and friends - send out change of address cards to any friends and relations missed first time around.

❏ Employer (they should tell the tax office and any other financial organisation such as a company pension body)

- ❏ Trade union or professional association
- ❏ TV licence
- ❏ Passport
- ❏ Driving licence (don't send this off before moving especially if you are hiring any vehicles; it is also a useful evidence of identity)
- ❏ Vehicle registration
- ❏ Vehicle insurance
- ❏ House contents insurance
- ❏ Life insurance and pension company
- ❏ School
- ❏ Optician
- ❏ Doctor
- ❏ Dentist
- ❏ Vet
- ❏ Blood transfusion centre
- ❏ Bank and credit card companies
- ❏ Store card companies
- ❏ Local authority (Council Tax)
- ❏ Electoral Register
- ❏ Subscriptions to magazines and catalogue companies
- ❏ Sports club and social associations
- ❏ Premium bonds

SETTLING INTO YOUR NEW HOME

- Have all your door locks changed.
- Improve security, fitting extra mortice locks and window locks. Contact the Crime Prevention Officer at your local police station for advice.
- Check how energy-conserving your new home is, and add extra insulation if necessary. A home-energy rating report will highlight deficiencies and recommend improvements (see page 129).
- If the previous owner has not arranged to have mail redirected, you could end up receiving all their 'junk' mail. To have the address

Energy Efficiency

Having an energy-rating assessment on your home will tell you how
efficient it is (or isn't) and where improvements can be made. The cost
effectiveness of different modifications is included in the assessment so
you can plan any improvements to take advantage of quick, cheap
alterations with instant pay-backs.

There is a Government-approved Standard Assessment Procedure
(SAP) which is used by two companies to carry out assessments.

MVM Starpoint charge £50 for a written report. On-the-spot advice
by the surveyor costs £10 extra.

The National Energy Services Ltd charge £50-£100 depending on the
size of the house and the assessor.

The assessments are useful in determining how much the house costs
to run and how savings can be made with pay-back forecasts.

If you are on income-related benefits from the state or over 60, you
may be eligible for assistance on home improvements such as insulation
and draughtproofing. Further details about the Home Energy Efficiency
Scheme can be obtained from the Energy Action Grants Agency.

removed, contact the Mailing Preference Service. They will return an
application form for you to complete.

- Consider taking out a home emergency insurance scheme. Both the
AA Homeline and Home Emergency Services offer a 'breakdown
service' for your home. They provide 24-hour cover with a helpline
and have approved contractors to help you out if you should have any
problems with central heating, plumbing or house structure such as
leaky roofing. Details of charges and cover are available from each
organisation.

- If you are considering any maintenance or improvement
work, contact the Fair Trades Advisory Bureau. It lists reputable
contractors and covers you for a refund if one of its members goes out
of business. Always use a firm which is insured by a company registered
with the Association of British Insurers, and which has a Public
Liability Insurance.

YOUR USEFUL CONTACTS

Estate Agent

Solicitor/Conveyancer

Removals firm

Insurance company

Building society

Bank

Credit Card company

Plumber

Electrician

Gas man

Water Company   old house

new house

Electricity company   old house

new house

Gas company   old house

new house

Council Tax   old house

new house

Telephone company

New school(s)

New doctor

New dentist

A.A./R.A.C.

USEFUL ADDRESSES

AA (Automobile Association) Homeline
Norfolk House
Priestley Road
Basingstoke
Hampshire RG24 9NY
Homeline: 01345 383838

Advisory Centre for Education (ACE)
22 Highbury Grove
16 Aberdeen Studios
London N5 2DQ
Telephone advice service available 2pm
to 5pm: 0171 354 8321

Architects and Surveyors Institute
15 St Mary Street
Chippenham
Wiltshire SN15 3WD
Telephone: 01249 444505

Associated Self Build Architects
No. 1, the Business Court
Bradford Road
East Arnsley
Leeds WS3 2AB
Freephone: 0800 387310

Association of British Insurers
51 Gresham Street
London EC2V 7HQ
Telephone: 0171 600 3333

Association of Building Engineers
Jubilee House
Billing Brook Road
Weston Favell
Northamptonshire NN3 8NW
Telephone: 01604 404121

Association of Relocation Agents
Premier House
11 Marlborough Place
Brighton BN1 1UB
Telephone: 01273 624455

Association of Selfbuilders
47a Brushfield Street
Old Spitalfields Market
London E1 6AA
Telephone: 0171 377 6763

Banking Ombudsman
70 Gray's Inn Road
London WC1X 8NB
Telephone: 0171 404 9944

Beco Products Ltd
Beco House
Wrawby Road
Brigg
South Humberside DN20 8DT
Telephone: 01652 651641

BergHus Europe Ltd
Gatwick Imperial Centre
43 Gatwick Road
Crawley
West Sussex RH10 2SD
Telephone: 01209 821805

Border Oak Design and Construction Ltd
Kingsland Sawmills
Kingsland
Leominster
Herefordshire HR6 9SF
Telephone: 01568 708752

Bradford & Bingley Building Society
PO Box 2, Main Street
Bingley
West Yorkshire BD16 2LW
Freephone: 0800 252993

British Association of Removers (BAR)
3 Churchill Court
58 Station Road
North Harrow
Middlesex HA2 7SA
Telephone: 0181 861 3331

The British Bankers' Association
10 Lombard Street
London EC3V 9EL
Telephone: 0171 623 4001

British Vehicle Rental and Leasing
  Association
13 St John's Street
Chichester
West Sussex PO19 1UU
Telephone: 01243 786782

Building Societies' Ombudsman
35-37 Grosvenor Gardens
London SW1X 7AW
Telephone: 0171 931 0044

Building Society Association/Council of
  Mortgage Lenders
3 Savile Row
London W1X 1AF
Telephone: 0171 437 0655

Cadw (Heritage Wales)
Welsh Historic Monuments
Brunel House
2 Fitzalan Road
Cardiff CF2 1UY
Telephone: 01222 500200

Carphone Warehouse
Rental Reservations: 0171 317 1224

Cheltenham & Gloucester Building
  Society
Chief Office
Barnett Way
Gloucester GL4 7RL
Freephone: 0800 272131

CNT (Commission for New Towns)
Saxon Court
502 Avebury Boulevard
Central Milton Keynes MK9 3HS
Telephone: 01908 696300

Constructive Individuals
47a Brushfield Street
Old Spitalfields Market
London E1 6AA
Telephone: 0171 377 6763

The Consumers' Association
(Which? Personal Service)
2 Marylebone Road
London NW1 4DF
Telephone: 0171 486 5544

Corporation of Insurance and Financial
    Advisors
174 High Street
Guildford
Surrey GU1 3HW
Telephone: 01483 39121

Council for Licensed Conveyancers
16 Glebe Road
Chelmsford CM1 1QG
Telephone: 01245 349599

Council for Registered Gas Installers
    (CORGI)
4 Elmwood, Chineham Business Park
Crockford Lane
Basingstoke
Hampshire RG24 8WG
Telephone: 01256 708133

Council of Mortgage Lenders
see Building Society Association

CREDIT REFERENCE AGENCIES
Equifax Europe (UK) Ltd
Consumer Affairs Department
Spectrum House
1A North Avenue
Clydebank
Glasgow G81 2DR

Infolink Ltd
CCA Department
38 Whitworth Street
Manchester M60 1QH

CCN Credit Systems
Consumer Affairs Department
PO BOX 40
Nottingham NG7 2SS

Credit Data and Marketing Services
CCA Department
Dove Mill
Dean Church Lane
Bolton
Lancashire BL3 4ET

Curtain Exchange
133 Stephendale Road
London SW6 2PG
Telephone: 0171 731 8316

Data Protection Registrar
Wycliffe House
Water Lane
Wilmslow
Cheshire SK9 5AF
Telephone: 01625 535711

Department of Environment leaflets
available from:
Department of Environment
PO Box 151
London E15 2HF
Fax: 0181 533 1618

Department of Environment Ireland
Historic Monuments
Commonwealth House
35 Castle Street
Belfast BT1 1GU
Telephone: 01232 314911

Design and Materials Ltd
Lawn Road
Carlton-in-Lindrick
Worksop
Nottinghamshire S81 9LB
Telephone: 01909 730333

DMS Services Ltd
Orchard House
Blyth
Worksop
Nottinghamshire S81 8HF
Telephone: 01909 591652

Energy Action Grants Agency
PO Box 1NG
Newcastle Upon Tyne NE1 7HA
Freephone: 0800 181667

English Heritage
23 Savile Row
London W1X 1AB
Advice line: 0171 973 3000

Fair Trades Advisory Bureau
The Quadrant
Hoylake
Wirral L47 2EE
Freephone: 0800 833 859

Georgian Group
37 Spital Square
London E1 6DY
Telephone: 0171 377 1722

Hang-ups Curtain Re-sale Agency
Telephone: 01489 798600

Heating and Ventilation Contractors
    Association
Esca House
34 Palace Court
London W2 4JG
Telephone: 0171 229 2488

Historic Scotland
Longmore House
Salisbury Place
Edinburgh EH9 1SH
Telephone 0131 668 8600

Home Emergency Services
PO Box 300
Leeds
West Yorkshire LS99 2LZ
Freephone: 0800 800688

Hosby Sale Ltd
Unit 24, The Nursery
High Street
Sutton Courtenay
Abingdon OX14 4UA
Telephone: 01235 848756

House Builder Federation
82 New Cavendish Street
London W1M 8AD
Telephone: 0171 580 5588

Independent Financial Advisors
    Association
12-13 Henrietta Street
Covent Garden
London WC2E 8LH
Telephone: 0171 240 7878

Independent Schools Information
Service (ISIS)
56 Buckingham Gate
London SW1E 6AG
Telephone: 0171 630 8793

Individual House Builders' Association
Telephone: 0753 621265

Incorporated Society of Valuers and
Auctioneers (ISVA)
3 Cadogan Gate
London SW1X 0AS
Telephone: 0171 235 2282

Institute of Plumbing
64 Station Lane
Hornchurch
Essex RM12 6NB
Telephone: 01708 472791

The Insurance Ombudsman
City-Gate 1
135 Park Street
London SE1 9EA
Telephone: 0171 928 7600

Investment Homes
Fairlight House
6 Andover Road
Newbury
Berkshire RG14 6LR
Telephone: 01635 521523

The Investment Ombudsman
6 Frederick's Place
London EC2R 8BT
Telephone: 0171 796 3065

Justice
11-12 Bouverie Street
London EC4Y 8BS

Landbank Services
PO Box 2035
Reading
Berkshire RG5 4YX
Telephone: 01734 310288

Land Tribunal for Scotland
1 Grosvenor Crescent
Edinburgh EH12 5ER
Telephone: 0131 225 7996

Law Society
113 Chancery Lane
London WC2A 1PL
Telephone: 0171 242 1222

Law Society Northern Ireland
Law Society House
98 Victoria Street
Belfast BT1 3JZ
Telephone: 01232 231614

Law Society of Scotland
26 Drumsheugh Gardens
Edinburgh EH3 7YR
Telephone: 0131 226 7411

Mailing Preference
Freepost 22
London W1E 7EZ

MVM Starpoint
MVM House
2 Oaklands Road
Bristol BS8 2AL
Telephone: 01179 250948

National Association of Estate Agents
Arbon House
21 Jury Street
Warwick CV34 4EH
Telephone: 01926 496800

National Energy Services Ltd
Rockingham Drive
Linford Wood
Milton Keynes MK14 6EG
Telephone: 01908 672787

National House-Building Council
Buildmark House
Chiltern Avenue
Amersham
Bucks HP6 5AP
Telephone: 01494 434477

National Inspection Council for
    Electrical Installation Contracting
    (NICEIC)
Vintage House
37 Albert Embankment
London SE1 7UJ
Telephone: 0171 582 7746

National Land Finding Agency
53 South Street
Bishops Stortford
Hertfordshire CM23 3AG
Telephone: 01279 461361

National Self Build Helpline
Telephone: 0181 549 2166
(11am-4pm)

New Homes Marketing Board
c/o House Builders Federation
82 New Cavendish Street
London W1M 8AD
Telephone: 0171 580 5588

Parcelforce
Redirection enquiries
Freephone: 0800 224466

Personal Investment Authority (PIA)
7th floor
1 Canada Square
Canary Wharf
London E14 5AZ
Telephone: 0171 538 8860

Potton Ltd
The Old Foundry
Willow Road
Potton
Bedfordshire SG19 2PP
Telephone: 01767 260348

Pre-school Learning Alliance
69 King's Cross Road
London WC1X 9LL
Telephone: 0171 833 0991

Royal Institute of British Architects
66 Portland Place
London W1N 4AD
Telephone: 0171 580 5533

Royal Institution of Chartered Surveyors
12 Great George Street
London SW1P 3AD
Helpline: 0171 222 7000

Royal Institution of Chartered Surveyors
  Scotland
9 Manor Place
Edinburgh EH3 7DN
Telephone: 0131 225 7078

Royal Mail
Mail redirection enquiries
Credit card payment: 0345 777 888

Ryder Truck Rental
Ryder House
16 Bath Road
Slough SL1 3SA
Freephone: 0800 100200

Ryton Books
29 Ryton Street
Worksop
Nottinghamshire S80 2AY
Telephone: 0909 591652

Scottish Civic Trust
24 George Street
Glasgow G21 1EF
Telephone: 0141 248 3398

Securities and Investment Board (SIB)
Gavrelle House
2-14 Bunhill Row
London EC1Y 8RA
Telephone: 0171 638 1240

Society for the Protection of Ancient
  Buildings
37 Spital Square
London E1 6DY
Telephone: 0171 377 1644

Ulster Architectural Heritage Society
185 Stranmillis Road
Belfast BT9 5DU
Telephone: 01232 660809

Victorian Society
1 Priory Gardens
Bedford Park
London W4 1TT
Telephone: 081 994 1019

Zurich Municipal (BGD)
Hermes House
Southwood Crescent
Farnborough
Hampshire GU14 0NJ
Telephone: 01252 522000

INDEX

completion dates, 109, 110, 112

conservation areas, 34, 36-7

contaminated land, 13

contents insurance, 21, 28, 70, 115-16

contracts:
  auctions, 111
  cohabitation, 21
  draft, 48, 49
  exchange of, 20, 48, 109
  in Scotland, 81

conveyancers, 12, 45-50, 88, 93, 99, 105

costs *see* finances

Council Tax, 26, 41, 51

cracks, 30, 54

credit reference agencies, 61

currency mortgages, 65

curtains, 121

Custom Build Guarantee, 101, 102

damp, 30, 53, 54

damp-proof course, 29-30

deeds, 74, 81, 84, 86

deposits, 56
  auctions, 23, 111
  conveyancers, 49
  estate agents, 11
  exchange of contracts, 109
  in Scotland, 81
  self-build companies, 99
  size of, 60-1

developers, mortgages, 44

disabled facilities grants, 33

discharge document, 86

discounts:
  mortgages, 66, 67
  right-to-buy scheme, 40

dishwashers, 16, 121

disposition, Scotland, 81, 86

DIY moving, 112-14

DIY selling, 82, 105-7

electricians, 121

electricity supplies, 26, 122, 126, 127

emergency insurance schemes, 129

employers, reference fees, 72

employer's liability insurance, 101

endowment mortgages, 44, 56, 62-3, 69, 71, 74, 75-6

energy ratings, 37-8, 128, 129

English Heritage, 34, 36

entry date, Scotland, 81, 85

estate agents, 50-2
  choosing, 51-2
  deposits, 11
  fees, 15, 51-2
  joint agents, 52
  mortgage brokers, 45, 59
  in Scotland, 78, 82, 83, 85
  and self-build houses, 91
  selling houses, 104-5, 107-8
  sole agency, 52
  valuations, 9

Estates Gazette, 22

exchange of contracts, 20, 48, 109

exchange of missives, 81, 85

exhibitions, self-build houses, 89

fees *see* finances

'feudal tenure', Scotland, 78

finances, 9-17
  auctions, 23, 110
  bridging loans, 11
  buying leases, 31
  costs in Scotland, 80
  Council Tax, 26, 41, 51
  deposits, 11, 60-1
  estate agents' fees, 51-2, 104-5
  grants, 33-4

Scotland, 34, 36, 77-86
Scottish Civic Trust, 32
searches, 13, 82
secondhand shops, 120
'Secured by Design' scheme, 38
Securities Investment Board, 76
security, 38, 128
self-build houses, 87-103
self-build property companies, 94-5, 96-9
selling possessions, 120
selling process:
    appealing to potential buyers, 107-8
    auctions, 110-11
    DIY, 82, 105-7
    estate agents, 104-5
    offers, 109
    in Scotland, 82-6
septic tanks, 25
service charges:
    flats, 27, 31, 41
    shared ownership, 42
services, charges, 26
sewers, 25
shared ownership, 41-2
Society for the Protection of Ancient
Buildings, 32
sole agency, 52
sole selling rights, 52
solicitors:
    conveyancing, 45-50
    fees, 12, 14
    in Scotland, 80-6
    searches, 13
    selling at auction, 110
solicitors' property centres, Scotland, 77, 83
Stamp Duty, 11, 31, 41, 48, 99
storage firms, 116-18
structural guarantees, self-build houses,

101-3
structural surveys, 13-14, 20, 53, 54-5, 80, 109
subcontractors, 93-4, 99, 103
subsidence, 30
survey fees, 72
surveyors, 30, 32-3, 53-5, 82, 109
surveys:
    Home Buyer's Survey and Valuation (HBSV), 13, 29, 53-4, 80
    in Scotland, 78
    structural, 13-14, 20, 53, 54-5, 80, 109
    valuation, 13, 20, 29, 53, 80, 82, 105-6, 109
survival kit, moving house, 125

taxation:
    cashback schemes, 67
    Council Tax, 26, 41, 51
    mortgage tax relief, 73
    VAT, 103, 104
telephone mortgage services, 58
telephones, 16, 122, 123, 124, 127
Teletext services, 38-9
tender, sale by, 23
term insurance, 70
tie-ins, mortgage lenders, 70-1
timber-framed houses, 95, 98
timber treatments, 30, 53
tipping, removal men, 127
title deeds, 74, 81, 84, 86
TransAction Protocol, 49
TV licences, 122, 128

unit-linked endowment mortgages, 62-3
unpacking, 127
utilities, charges, 26

valuation: